Network+ All-in-One Lab Manual

About the Author

Catherine Creary (Independent Technical Trainer, entrepreneur, and writer) currently holds a Bachelor of Education, MCT, MCSE, and MCDBA. She has over 12 years of experience in the field of education. Catherine is the author of numerous training courses (Digital Think), an Exchange 2000 columnist (www.OutlookExchange.com), and author of several articles regarding Cross Border Employment for IT personnel. She has extensive experience in computer training, including development of adult education computer courses and curriculum design.

Network+ All-in-One Lab Manual

Catherine Creary

McGraw-Hill/Osborne

New York Chicago San Francisco Lisbon London Madrid
Mexico City Milan New Delhi San Juan Seoul Singapore
Sydney Toronto

McGraw-Hill/Osborne
2600 Tenth Street
Berkeley, California 94710
U.S.A.

To arrange bulk purchase discounts for sales promotions, premiums, or fund-raisers, please contact **McGraw-Hill**/Osborne at the above address. For information on translations or book distributors outside the U.S.A., please see the International Contact Information page immediately following the index of this book.

Network+ All-in-One Lab Manual

234567890 DOC DOC 019876543

ISBN 0-07-219522-3

Publisher
Brandon A. Nordin

Vice President & Associate Publisher
Scott Rogers

Acquisitions Editor
Chris Johnson

Project Managers
Deidre Dolce
Jenn Tust

Freelance Project Managers
Tory McLearn
Laurie Stewart

Acquisitions Coordinator
Athena Honore

Technical Editor
Don Fisher

Copy Editor
Kim Goodfriend

Proofreader
Andrea Fox

Indexer
Jack Lewis

Computer Designer
Jeffrey Wilson, Happenstance Type-O-Rama

Illustrator
Jeffrey Wilson, Happenstance Type-O-Rama

Series Design
Maureen Forys, Happenstance Type-O-Rama

Cover Design
Patti Lee

This book was composed with QuarkXPress 4.11 on a Macintosh G4.

To my parents—thank you for helping me discover and know my life's true purpose.

Dad, your devotion and discipline inspire me. Mom, your strength and passion encourage me.

To Dean—thank you for your endless support and presence in my life. Thank you for telling me time and time again, "You can do it."

Contents

Acknowledgments

Thanks first and foremost to Chris Johnson, Athena Honore, and all the others at **McGraw-Hill**/Osborne who worked hard putting this book together. A thanks to Don Fisher for his invaluable technical edits.

Thanks to my agent Neil Salkind of Studio B Productions Ltd. (www.studiob.com), Craig Wiley, Krystin Pickens, and all the staff at Studio B for their fantastic representation of so many wonderful authors. I'm proud to be a part of your team.

Thanks to Ken Symes, who provided me with Network+ tips and a lot of laughs, mostly at my expense!

Thanks to Tory McLearn, Laurie Stewart, Jeffrey Wilson, Maureen Forys, and Andrea Fox at Happenstance for their editorial and production assistance.

Thanks to my mentor in this crazy IT business, Mitch Tulloch (www.mtit.com), in whose footsteps I follow. I thank God for providing me someone who, in addition to offering solid professional advice, is an outstanding human being to know.

Introduction

Welcome to the lab manual that accompanies your *All-in-One Network+ Certification Exam Guide* (McGraw-Hill/Osborne, 2002). The lab manual is organized into chapters that map to the chapters of the textbook. There may be several lab exercises per chapter.

Each chapter will include a chapter introduction, a material list, and setup instructions for each lab as well as the lab exercises. The labs themselves include hands-on activities, network design problems, and troubleshooting questions that may require research by you, the reader. The labs will not only prepare you for the Network+ exam but also will prepare you for possible real-life scenarios that you may encounter at a variety of IT jobs.

Each chapter also has five Lab Analysis questions and a Key Term Quiz that allow you to demonstrate your knowledge of the material covered in the chapter. Finally, the chapter concludes with a brief summary of the key points. Step-by-step solutions to the labs are provided for all chapters and are found at the end of each chapter.

Chapter 1

Introduction

Lab Exercise

Welcome to the *Network+ All-in-One Lab Manual!* The focus of this book is to provide possible real-life scenarios that you, the reader, may come across in the future—whether you're working as a systems administrator for a large corporation, a technical support specialist for a medium-sized company, or a network engineer/jack-of-all-trades for a small business.

This book is part of McGraw-Hill/Osborne's All-in-One series that includes the *Network+ All-in-One Certification Exam Guide, Second Edition,* the textbook that teaches the networking concepts and terms you'll need to know to complete the labs included here. Both books are organized in 21 chapters, the lab manual chapters mapping to the chapters of the textbook.

Learning About Life on the Job

This manual provides case studies that allow you to learn by practice, so that you can apply what the *Network+ All-in-One Certification Exam Guide* has introduced to network scenarios. Readers can use their own computer systems and network hardware to simulate real-life scenarios. This book is designed for readers in both a home network and/or classroom environment. Additionally, screen shots and other illustrations are also included to make this book an excellent learning tool for those readers who may not have the hardware to set up their own networks.

These chapters include step-by-step hands-on labs, teaching you how to install and configure a network environment as well as design labs that allow you to plan for future installations. This book also includes Lab Analysis questions and a Key Term Quiz in every chapter. Readers who are preparing for the Network+ Certification Exam will find this book a valuable resource for understanding the concepts and terminology of networking, through actively performing the hands-on, network tasks that you will encounter on the job.

There are no prerequisites for taking the Network+ Certification Exam in terms of networking experience or training courses. If you simply want to pass the exam, you can study the written words, memorize the terminology, and even guess your way through the multiple-choice questions. But if you want to learn to be an effective administrator, technician, or engineer, the way to do so is through doing the work!

Have you ever thought about what skills you will need to acquire to effectively administer a Novell network? What about a Microsoft network? What if you were offered a job as a technical support specialist? What problems might you encounter with a large network, as opposed to a small network environment?

If you're not already working day-to-day in the computer field, you may not realize what day-to-day tasks you may encounter, and what skills you may need to acquire before successfully obtaining a job in the IT industry. In terms of designing, administering, maintaining, and troubleshooting network environments, you will have to know all of the information included in this manual.

For example, a systems administrator may need to understand the overall design and cabling topology of the network he or she is administering, while a technical support specialist may have to concentrate on supporting computer hardware and troubleshooting network connectivity. All of these concepts are included on the Network+ Certification Exam. The exam will test you on the different network cabling topologies, hardware, cabling types, and protocols. Each Network+ test candidate should be able to install and configure a PC in a small or large network environment.

In summary, you can think of the exam as an opportunity to prove your knowledge of networking concepts and tasks, as well as a means of obtaining an industry-recognized certification.

 30 MINUTES

Lab 1.01: Seeing Your Future

You are considering a career in the IT industry. You know very little about the jobs available in the industry or the different responsibilities of each occupational title. You decide to research the industry before making your final decision.

Learning Objectives

In this exercise, you'll learn the exciting challenges and rewards available to you on completion of this course. When you complete this exercise, you will be able to

- Recognize IT job occupations
- Describe the typical job responsibilities of a network administrator
- Define the salary ranges for different IT occupations

Lab Materials and Setup

For this lab exercise, you'll need

- Paper and pencil
- Internet access

Getting Down to Business

Step 1   List at least five Information Technology occupations.

_____

_____

Step 2   What are the job responsibilities of a network administrator?

_____

_____

Step 3   What is the average salary for a network administrator in your local town or city?

_____

_____

Step 4   Use the Internet to research the average salary for at least three occupations in the IT industry.

Solution

In this section, you'll find the solution to the lab exercise.

Lab 1.01 Solution

Answers will vary for the questions; however, these web sites will provide additional information:

Step 1   www.workfutures.bc.ca/EN/def/doc/comp_e1.html

Step 2   linux.oreillynet.com/pub/a/linux/2000/07/20/LinuxAdmin.html

Steps 3 and 4   www.datamasters.com/survey.html

Chapter 2
Networking Fundamentals

Lab Exercises

Networking, as we know it today, has gone through many changes. There have been several types of networks since the first computers were linked together to share information. To understand today's network scenarios, it is helpful to understand the networks of the past decades. These labs will enable you to compare and contrast network environments. You will learn to recognize the main components of a network. You will also design a network solution for a small business environment and share network resources.

 20 MINUTES

Lab 2.01: Examining the History of Networking

The employees of Datatemp, Inc., began their company with one mainframe computer that allowed users access to data on the mainframe's storage device. This scenario was slow and did not allow users to share information from their individual terminals. Datatemp's goal was to allow employees in the Chicago office to share information with users in the Denver office. The process of sharing data between mainframe computers in each city was a concept that Datatemp was considering but had not yet implemented. This scenario would allow the mainframe computers to share resources but would not meet the users' needs of sharing information from their individual terminals. Datatemp had to implement a network solution that would satisfy the needs of its employees.

Learning Objectives

In this lab, you'll examine network infrastructures and suggest a network solution. At the end of this lab, you will be able to

- Recognize a mainframe computer system
- Illustrate the need for networks
- Explain networking concepts

Lab Materials and Setup

For this lab exercise, you'll need

- Pencil and paper

Getting Down to Business

Step 1 Describe the limitations of a stand-alone mainframe computer that is not in a networked environment.

_____

_____

Step 2 Briefly explain how networking mainframe computers can increase productivity for Datatemp, Inc., employees between Chicago and Denver.

_____

_____

Step 3 Suggest a modern-day network solution that would satisfy the needs of Datatemp, Inc., employees.

_____

_____

 15 MINUTES

Lab 2.02: Designing a Network

Western Supply Company is a small manufacturer of pet supplies. Their office employs 3 managers and 30 staff employees. The current needs of the company are data storage, e-mail communication, and remote access by several traveling employees to the company network. Western Supply has hired you to design a basic network scenario that would suit the needs of the company.

Learning Objectives

In this lab, you'll design a network solution for a small business. At the end of this lab, you will be able to

- Recognize the computer roles on a network
- Analyze the needs of a small business
- Design a network solution

Lab Materials and Setup

For this lab, you'll need

- Pencil and paper

Getting Down to Business

Step 1   A manager has impressed on you the immediate need for a central location for data storage for all employees. In the following space, describe a quick solution to this problem.

_____

_____

Step 2 Several employees from the company need to access their e-mail and other files from remote locations. Suggest a solution based on your knowledge of older technologies. How might you update a network solution based on an older technology to meet Western Supply Co.'s needs?

_____

_____

Step 3 Design a network environment that would accommodate 3 managers, 30 employees, and provide centralized data storage, e-mail communication, remote access, and shared resources. List the number of client computers and servers that would accommodate the needs of Western Supply Co.

_____

_____

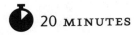 20 MINUTES

Lab 2.03: Sharing Network Resources

Lucas High School has hired you as a resource librarian. Your main responsibility is to establish a plan for sharing the school library's catalog of book titles with all teacher and student computers on the school network. You will need to determine where to store the catalog of titles and how to share the list effectively and efficiently to the entire staff and student population.

Learning Objectives

In this lab, you'll examine the process of sharing network resources. At the end of this lab, you will be able to

- Recognize the need for sharing resources

- Determine where to store shared data

- Share files and access shared resources

Lab Materials and Setup

For this lab exercise, you'll need

- Pencil and paper

Getting Down to Business

Step 1   The school principal has asked you to make the catalog of book titles available to the entire school population. You examine the school network and discover that you have five library client computers, ten staff computers located in various offices and staff rooms, and ten student computers located in the student resource center that are available for public use. What network scenario would you implement to share the catalog of titles and what, if any, computers should be added to the school's current network infrastructure?

_____

_____

Step 2 Suggest a storage location for the catalog of titles. Compare the effects of storing the catalog on several computers versus one centralized location.

_____

_____

Step 3 Describe the visual and practical effects to the local computers when sharing the catalog of titles with the entire school population.

_____

_____

✔ **Hint**

What visual changes occur on the resource being shared? Does the icon look the same as it did before it was shared? Will users have to access the resource from its stored physical location or can they access the resource across the network?

Lab Analysis

1. You determine that your boss needs to access the documents that you created and saved on your computer's hard drive. How can you utilize your network environment to enable your boss to retrieve these documents easily?

    _____

    _____

2. You have been assigned the task of explaining the concept of networking to a new employee at your company who is unfamiliar with how computers share information. What will you tell this new employee to help him understand the types and functions of computer systems on your network?

    _____

    _____

3. What is the main purpose of a server in a client/server environment?

    _____

    _____

4. What types of networks preceded client/server networks?

    _____

    _____

5. What types of resources can be shared in a network environment?

    _____

    _____

Key Term Quiz

Use the following vocabulary terms to complete the sentences below. Not all of the terms will be used.

ARPANET

client

CRT terminal

mainframe computers

remote terminals

resource

server

software

1. A _____ is an item or device on a network that can be shared with other systems.

2. _____ was the first practical network created by the Advanced Research Project Agency.

3. Large computers that processed information from punch cards or magnetic tape and required long periods of time to produce results were know as _____.

4. A _____ is a computer system on a network that accesses a shared resource.

5. A _____ is a computer system on a network that shares resources.

Lab Wrap-Up

The sharing of information is crucial to business operations. Networks provide the ability to share information on powerful servers allowing client systems to access files, folders, printers, and other resources. This chapter provided an introduction to networking concepts and functions. You have now successfully analyzed present and past network infrastructures, designed a network solution, and shared resources in a client/server environment.

Solutions

In this section, you'll find solutions to the lab exercises, the Lab Analysis questions, and the Key Term Quiz.

Lab 2.01 Solution

Step 1   A stand-alone mainframe computer is sometimes a slow computer system that only allows users to access common data on the system and provides no sharing of information between systems. Most mainframe computers were also accessed using punch cards and took hours or days to process a user's request for data. Prior to personal computers, these large mainframe computers served multiple users who logged onto the mainframe at dumb terminals. Software applications were stored on disks attached to the mainframe computer. This allowed multiple users to share applications while they shared the same CPU. A disadvantage was that if one user ran a CPU-intensive job, this would negatively affect the performance of all other users' jobs.

Step 2   Networking the mainframe computers in Chicago and Denver would provide shared information between the two mainframe computers, allowing users in Chicago to access data that was originally stored on Denver's mainframe. However, Datatemp employees would still not be able to share data from their individual terminals. In the mainframe systems, there is a solution to this shared data problem. This is solved if Datatemp, Inc., used a smart terminal rather than a dumb terminal; files can be shared via standard TCP/IP protocols such as FTP for sharing files between the two smart terminals. However, both terminals would have to be smart terminals, which have their own operating system and storage devices on the local machine.

Step 3   Implementing a client/server network environment would allow users of Datatemp, Inc., to share data on their individual computers as well as store data on the Chicago and Denver servers for use by all clients in both cities. This would be the most efficient method of sharing information and would satisfy the needs of Datatemp, Inc., employees. The client/server network would not only need to implement either a local area networks (LAN) or wide area network (WAN), but also several network protocols and hardware devices to provide communication. Consider how any potential design strategy must include these additional elements.

Lab 2.02 Solution

Step 1   Implement a server that allows for centralized data storage for all managers and employees. Organize file storage for individual users and allow all client computers to access this server.

Step 2   Establish an e-mail server that would meet the needs of e-mail communication. Establish a remote access solution, based on the remote terminal networks of the past that would allow users to dial in from client computers outside the network environment to access data on the server. Update this solution by allowing clients to share data from their remote computers.

Step 3   Install 33 client computers that would accommodate each individual user and manager. Install one or more centralized servers for e-mail communication, data storage, and remote access. Allow all clients, both on the local and remote networks, the ability to connect to all servers in the network environment. Allow all clients to share data on their individual client computers and on the network servers. The installation of more than one server would provide for fault tolerance in case of server failure, as well as provide load balancing for the various services offered to connected clients. Load balancing allows for several servers to provide individual services so that one server does not carry the load of client connections and processing. A load balancing solution would be to provide a mail server for e-mail communication, a file/application server for data storage, and a remote access server for remote client connections.

Lab 2.03 Solution

Step 1   Implement a client/server network scenario by adding a server to the school network and enable access to this server from all client computers.

Step 2   Store the catalog of titles on the centralized server, so that client computers can connect to the server and gain access to the catalog. This solution provides easy access without the need for installing the catalog of titles on each individual client computer in the school, which would take more time and resources.

Step 3   Once you share a resource on a computer the icon representing the resource changes its look. Resources can be shared on a variety of operating systems, including Macintosh, Linux, UNIX, and Windows. In the case of a Windows operating system, the shared resource will have the added effect of an outstretched hand to the icon. The entire school population will be able to access the resource from a connection across the network, acting as if it were locally stored on the client computer's hard drive.

Answers to Lab Analysis

1.   You can utilize the client/server network environment by either storing the documents on the server in a shared location accessible by your boss, or you can store the documents

on your local computer's hard drive and share the files, giving your boss adequate permission to obtain access.

2. Explain to him/her that all employees are able to create, save, and share documents and other resources either in a central location (server) or locally on their computer's storage device. Explain that through the network environment, users are able to connect to either the server or other client computers to obtain access to the shared resources.

3. A server is a powerful computer that is used as a central device for data and other shared resources, which all client computers can access. Using the server as a central device is preferred, as not all servers are centrally located in a physical location.

4. Mainframe networks are two or more mainframe computers sharing resources with each other. Remote terminal networks are remote terminals connecting to mainframe systems to access shared data. ARPANET networks are client computers sharing information with mainframe servers.

5. Files, folders, and printers are examples of resources that can be shared in a network environment. Additional resources may include CD-ROM towers, scanners, modem pools, routers, and gateways.

Answers to Key Term Quiz

1. resource

2. ARPANET

3. mainframe computers

4. client

5. server

Chapter 3
Building a Network with OSI

Lab Exercises

The process of delivering data across a network from one computer to another may seem simple to the user. For example, a user attaches a photo image to an e-mail and sends it to a friend, who, in turn, receives the e-mail message, opens it with a mail program, and views the photo. What actually happens to this simple mail message and photo from sender to recipient is a complex process utilizing hardware, software, and various network protocols. In this chapter, you will analyze the many layers of data transfer through several lab scenarios.

 15 MINUTES

Lab 3.01: Utilizing the Network Hardware

Symes & Sons, a small interior design firm, has recently hired you as a technical support specialist. Your first project is to ensure that several user workstations have the correct configuration for future installation on the company network. The current network scenario implements a physical star topology with a central hub to which all computers connect. You must determine whether you possess the appropriate hardware to connect these workstations to the current network.

Learning Objectives

In this lab, you'll examine network infrastructures and suggest a network solution. At the end of this lab, you will be able to

- Recognize network hardware components
- Execute various Windows commands that render vital network information

Lab Materials and Setup

For this lab exercise, you'll need

- Pencil and paper
- Internet access

- Computer with a network operating system and NIC installed (Windows 9x, Windows NT 4.0, Windows 2000, or Windows XP will suffice)

- Various network cables (coaxial and UTP)

- Active hub (optional)

Getting Down to Business

Step 1   Identify the network interface card (NIC) located on the back of your local PC. In the following space, note the type of network cable that is connected to the PC's NIC.

_____

_____

Step 2   Perform the following steps:

a)   Boot the computer.

b)   Log on to the computer if prompted.

c)   Open a command prompt (also known as the DOS prompt) window.

d)   At the command prompt type **IPCONFIG /ALL** (if you have Windows NT/2000) or **WINIPCFG** (if you have Windows 95/98).

What type of information is displayed when using these commands?

_____

_____

Step 3   In the following space, write down the physical address for your local PC.

_____

_____

Step 4   Besides using the ipconfig and/or winipcfg command, how else can you identify the MAC address if the PC is not running or is disabled?

_____

_____

✔ **Hint**

When the PC is not running or is disabled, there is no operating system available to query hardware devices.

Step 5   In the following space, write the IP address for the computer. What is the naming convention of a standard IP address? Does your IP address fit this naming convention?

_____

_____

Step 6   Connecting computers to the Symes & Sons network requires additional configuration beyond setting up the physical hardware and cabling. What additional components do you need to install on the workstations for them to become networked? Research on the Internet to determine the necessary components for installing a Windows 2000 Professional computer on a network with Windows 2000 Servers running the TCP/IP protocol.

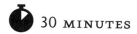 30 MINUTES

Lab 3.02: Understanding the Data Delivery Process

Dean wants to use the company network to access an image file located on his co-worker George's computer. The network is made up of computers running several different operating systems (Novell, UNIX, and Windows), all communicating through the TCP/IP protocol. Dean browses the network and connects to George's computer, then accesses the shared folder in which the image is located. He then attempts to open the image file from this location so that it is viewable on his computer. Dean is able to view the image through an application on his computer, yet he is unsure of how the data was actually transferred to his computer. He asks for your help in understanding the process of data delivery.

Learning Objectives

In this lab, you'll examine the process of data delivery on a network. You will also identify the components involved in transferring data between two computers on a network. At the end of this lab, you will be able to

- Identify the parts of a data frame
- Examine the process of data packet delivery

Lab Materials and Setup

For this lab exercise, you'll need

- Pencil and paper
- Internet access

Getting Down to Business

Step 1 Based on your knowledge of TCP data packets, list and define the parts of a generic TCP packet. Use the Internet to assist you in defining each part of a packet.

Step 2   Based on your knowledge of frames, list and define the parts of an IP packet in a frame. Use the Internet to assist you in defining each part of a frame.

_____

_____

Step 3   In the following space, briefly describe the process of data delivery from George's computer to Dean's computer, based on your knowledge of packets and frames.

_____

_____

 45 MINUTES

Lab 3.03: Examining the OSI Layers

DGK Enterprises has hired you to train the help desk and technical support staff on the various protocols involved in data transfer and communication. You have decided to use the OSI layer model to help explain the process to the staff. You must ensure that you can effectively demonstrate the relationship between the protocols and layers of the model.

Learning Objectives

In this lab, you'll examine the layers of the OSI model. At the end of this lab, you will be able to

- Identify and define the seven OSI layers

- Recognize the protocols that function at each OSI layer

- Analyze a networking task according to the OSI layers

Lab Materials and Setup

For this lab exercise, you'll need

- Pencil and paper

- Internet access

Getting Down to Business

Step 1 List the seven layers of the OSI model in the following chart and include the protocols that function at each layer. Include a brief description of the function of each layer. Use the Internet to assist you in your research.

OSI Layer	Protocols	Function
_____	_____	_____
_____	_____	_____
_____	_____	_____
_____	_____	_____
_____	_____	_____
_____	_____	_____
_____	_____	_____

Step 2   The help desk staff supports multiple users who connect to FTP servers over the Internet through FTP clients to transfer text files and images. Briefly describe the communication and data transfer process of a text file from the client application to the server, using the OSI layers and protocols.

_____

_____

Lab Analysis

1. What layer of the OSI model turns binary code into a physical signal?

_____

_____

2. What is the purpose of data encryption when sending data across the Internet?

_____

_____

3. Which physical device creates and destroys data frames on a network?

_____

_____

4. At which layer of the OSI model would the FTP protocol operate?

_____

_____

5. Which level of the OSI model is responsible for breaking data up and putting it back together?

_____

_____

Key Term Quiz

Use the following vocabulary terms to complete the sentences below. Not all of the terms will be used.

   broadcast address

   cyclical redundancy check (CRC)

   frame

   IPCONFIG /ALL

   MAC address

   network interface card (NIC)

   network protocol

   router

   TCP/IP

   WINIPCFG

1. A _____ is a container for data packets moving across a network.

2. Running the _____ command on a Windows 2000 computer will display the MAC address of the computer's network interface card.

3. The _____ is the portion of a frame that a NIC uses to determine whether data in the received frame is valid.

4. To simultaneously send the same message to multiple recipients would require sending it to a _____.

5. A physical address is another name for the _____ of a NIC.

Lab Wrap-Up

We now know that the data delivery process includes utilizing hardware, software, and various network protocols. The seven layers of the OSI model can sum up this process. The applications and protocols that function at the different layers of the model enable the data to travel through each layer, from source to destination computer. The networking industry uses the OSI model to describe functions such as turning binary data into electrical signals, identifying devices on the network, routing data packets, breaking up data packets and putting them back together, and managing connections between computers. As you can see, these are the many tasks that happen when a computer on a network attempts a simple task of transferring a file. Keep this in mind and you will have no problem understanding the importance of the OSI model.

Solutions

In this section, you'll find solutions to the lab exercises, the Lab Analysis questions, and the Key Term Quiz.

Lab 3.01 Solution

Step 1   The NIC and hub should both be able to connect to a UTP cable with an RJ-45 connector. This connector resembles the RJ-11 connectors used for telephone cables.

Step 2   The IPCONFIG /ALL and WINIPCFG commands display configuration information for each adapter bound to TCP/IP. This includes the IP address, subnet mask, default gateway, physical address, host name, and several other configuration parameters.

Step 3   The physical address is indicated by the 12-digit/character combination (xx-xx-xx-xx-xx-xx) in the Adapter section of the command prompt window. Ethernet adapters are the most common type of adapter available today. There are other types of adapters (such as Token Ring) that you may encounter; however, a MAC address is common to all adapters. This address is unique to each network card; therefore, answers will vary.

Step 4   You will also find the physical address written on the network interface card installed in your computer.

Step 5   The IP address of computers will vary. The standard naming convention for an IP address is four numbers (between 0 and 255) separated by periods. Your IP address should fit this naming convention.

Step 6   Aside from having the necessary hardware, a Windows 2000 Professional computer's LAN connection must have a network protocol installed to communicate with the Windows 2000 Server. In this case, the network protocol used is TCP/IP, as the server supports this protocol. The Windows 2000 Professional computer must also have a client service installed. In this case, the client service is Client for Microsoft Networks, as it can be used to connect to a Windows 2000 Server. If file or printer sharing is desired, then the client service (File and Printer Sharing for Microsoft Networks) must also be installed on the Windows 2000 Professional computer.

Lab 3.02 Solution

Step 1

> **Source port** is the protocol port or endpoint to a connection that is identified with an application protocol. The port number identifies what type of port is being used, for example FTP – port 21. This port represents the computer sending the data.

> **Destination port** represents the application protocol on the computer receiving the data.

> **Sequence number** is a number assigned to a packet to identify it from other packets broken down and delivered across the network that need to be reassembled.

> **Acknowledgement number** is a number assigned to a packet that identifies the packet receipt at the destination.

> **Data** is the image, text, audio, or other data type being delivered.

Step 2

> **Frame** is a container that envelopes packets sent across the network wires.

> **Packet** refers to the protocol packet (TCP, IP, and so on) for delivery.

> **Data** is the image, text, audio, video, or other data type destined for delivery.

> **CRC** is a technique used for checking data through a mathematical calculation to verify that data was received correctly.

Step 3   The first step in packet delivery from George's computer to Dean's computer is the process of chopping the image data into several packets (approximately 1,000 to 1,500 bytes in size for a typical packet). Each packet is assigned a sequence number so that Dean's computer will be able to assemble the packets into a readable image once they arrive. Each packet is also assigned the MAC address of both George's and Dean's computer. The packets are then sent to the NIC on George's computer for transfer and that NIC adds a frame around the packet, which also contains both the sender's and recipient's MAC addresses and the cyclical redundancy check. Each frame is then sent off to its destination by the best available route, after the NIC makes sure that the network wire is available (not busy) for data delivery. Each computer on the network receives each frame, but only Dean's computer, which has the correct MAC address indicated on the NIC, will process the frames. Dean's NIC organizes the frames based on their sequence numbers, uses the cyclical redundancy check to verify that the data received is valid, strips off the frame, and sends the data to the operating system for processing. Dean's computer is then able to view the image through an appropriate application.

Lab 3.03 Solution

Step 1

OSI Layer	Protocols	Function
Application	SMB, NCP	Allows applications to use the network
Presentation	NCP	Translates and encrypts data
Session	NetBIOS, Named Pipes	Establishes sessions by applications on separate computers
Transport	TCP, UDP, SPX, NetBEUI, NWLink	Packet handling and error-free delivery
Network	IP, IPX, NetBEUI, NWLink, DLC	Addresses and routes messages
Data Link	N/A	Manages physical layer data between connected systems
Physical	N/A	Transmits data over physical medium

Step 2 The FTP application begins the process of transferring a file to the FTP server. This process begins at the Application layer of the OSI model. The text file is then translated into a format that can be read through the receiving server, if necessary. This Presentation layer function is often ignored in modern operating systems. The connection is then established between the client and server at the Session layer of the model. The Transport layer breaks up the text file into smaller data pieces (packets) for transport. The addressing and routing information is added to the packets at the Network layer and the NIC identifies whether the network is busy or free to deliver the packet. If the packet can be delivered, the Physical layer is used to transmit the data over the physical cables. The packet should then arrive at the FTP server, and the OSI layers will be accessed in reverse, stripping off layers of the frame until the destination computer can view the data.

Answers to Lab Analysis

1. The Physical layer turns binary code into a physical signal and then back into the 1s and 0s of binary code.

2. Encryption translates data into secret codes, preventing unauthorized viewing by hackers when sent across the Internet. This data can be decrypted at the destination through the use of a secret key or password.

3. The NIC of a computer is responsible for creating and destroying data frames on a network. It puts the MAC addresses and the CRC in the frame to ensure delivery to the correct recipient computer.

4. The FTP protocol is found at the Application layer of the OSI model. FTP is an application protocol used on the Internet for sending files.

5. The Transport layer is responsible for breaking up the data it receives from upper layers into smaller packets for transport and also putting the data back together once all packets are received at the destination computer.

Answers to Key Term Quiz

1. frame

2. IPCONFIG /ALL

3. cyclical redundancy check (CRC)

4. broadcast address

5. MAC address

Chapter 4

Hardware Concepts

Lab Exercises

Network design and cabling are extremely important in ensuring that data travels successfully from one computer to another. To understand today's network scenarios, you must understand the topology—how computers connect to each other. These labs will help you understand various network topologies and compare the cabling hardware that provides data transfer. You will also apply your knowledge of cabling and topology by designing a network solution.

 15 MINUTES

Lab 4.01: Understanding Network Topologies

Prayias International has hired you as a consultant to analyze their current network and make suggestions to improve performance. Prayias International currently has three offices in New York City that include the corporate headquarters and two branch offices. One branch office has implemented a standard star topology; the other has implemented a bus topology network. The corporate headquarters has implemented a ring topology network. The goal of Prayias International is to implement one standard topology that can combine each location into a single LAN. Figure 4-1 shows Prayias International's current network environment.

Learning Objectives

In this lab, you'll examine several network topologies. At the end of this lab, you will be able to

- Recognize the communication method of standard topologies

- Identify the advantages and disadvantages of selected topologies

- Suggest a topology that will satisfy the needs of a large corporation

Lab Materials and Setup

For this lab exercise, you'll need

- Pencil and paper

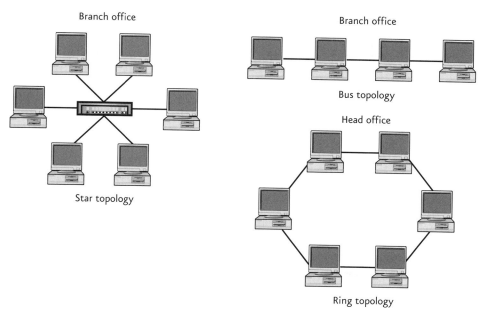

FIGURE 4-1 Prayias International's network

Getting Down to Business

Step 1 In the following space, describe the physical star, bus, and ring topologies and the method of communication between clients on these networks.

_____

_____

_____

Step 2 When comparing the star topology with the bus and ring topologies, what are the advantages and disadvantages of each?

_____

_____

_____

Step 3   What other topologies are available for Prayias International to consider?

_____

_____

✔ **Hint**

Hybrid topologies combine standard topologies to eliminate communication problems and improve the stability of data transfer.

Step 4   Suggest a hybrid topology that would solve most communication problems and satisfy the needs of Prayias International.

_____

_____

 20 MINUTES

Lab 4.02: Examining and Comparing Cabling

Greening Antiques is in the midst of establishing their first network of computers. Their goal is to install ten Windows 2000 Servers and 200 Windows 2000 Professional clients in a star bus topology network. They have hired you to suggest and implement a cabling solution that will be inexpensive and allow for reliable data transfer across the LAN.

Learning Objectives

In this lab, you'll learn to recognize and compare network cables. At the end of this lab, you will be able to

- Identify the various network cabling options

- Compare the function, speed, and maximum data transfer distance of each cable

- Suggest a cost-efficient cabling option for a medium-sized network

Lab Materials and Setup

For this lab exercise, you'll need

- Pencil and paper

- One RG-58 coaxial cable (no connector)

- One unshielded twisted-pair (UTP) cable (any category) and one shielded twisted-pair (STP) cable (optional)

- Fiber optic cable

- Internet access

Getting Down to Business

Step 1   Examine the various network cables in your possession and identify them by name.

_____

_____

Step 2   Note the appearance of each cable and describe any connectors on each cable end.

_____

_____

Step 3   Identify and note any category or other markings on the cables.

_____

_____

Step 4   What is the category of your UTP cable? What is the maximum speed of data transfer for each UTP category? Use the Internet to obtain the specifications of each cable type and note your findings.

_____

_____

Step 5   Greening Antiques estimates that the average data transfer rate for their network will be 100 Mbps. What cabling options will accommodate this data transfer rate? If Greening Antiques' network does not reach the 100 Mbps optimum bandwidth, as is common in the practical world, what factors may be responsible for the slowdown in throughput? Research this topic on the Internet and provide your answers here.

_____

_____

Step 6   Choose a cabling option for Greening Antiques that will meet their requirements and indicate the reasons for your choice.

_____

_____

 20 MINUTES

Lab 4.03: Establishing Network Connectivity

Sam and Emily's restaurant chain has expanded to include four additional locations in Boston, Montreal, Dallas, and New Orleans. The chain currently maintains two locations in New York City and Chicago. These four new locations will contain computers that will be added to the corporate wide area network (WAN). Sam and Emily's currently runs a mesh topology exclusively within each of the two existing locations. Both locations are installed as segments on the WAN connected to each other by an Ethernet backbone. The four new locations will also be added as segments connected to the Ethernet backbone. All segments encompass only workstation computers. Servers on the WAN are connected directly to the backbone and aren't involved in the mesh topology.

Learning Objectives

In this lab, you'll analyze and design a company network topology. At the end of this lab, you will be able to

- Illustrate a network scenario design

- Analyze a WAN with a dedicated backbone infrastructure

- Design a network topology solution

Lab Materials and Setup

For this lab exercise, you'll need

- Pencil and paper

- Internet access

Getting Down to Business

Step 1   Draw a design that encompasses Sam and Emily's current network infrastructure.

Step 2   Suggest a more efficient network topology for Sam and Emily's to replace their current mesh topology at each location. Indicate the advantages associated with your suggested topology and the disadvantages of Sam and Emily's current mesh topology. Why is the mesh topology rarely encountered in today's business environment?

_____

_____

Step 3   Indicate the UTP cabling options available for each restaurant location, based on the minimum speed of data transfer in the following table.

Restaurant Location	Minimum Data Transfer Speed	UTP Category
New York City	20 Mbps	_____
Chicago	16 Mbps	_____
Boston	10 Mbps	_____
Montreal	100 Mbps	_____
New Orleans	4 Mbps	_____

Step 4   Without changing the backbone infrastructure, will your new topology and cabling suggestions enable effective data transfer? Why?

_____

_____

Step 5   Why would it be advantageous to use a Category 5 UTP cabling plant to support all of the above data rates? In other words, why not use the lower category for the 4 Mbps, 10 Mbps, 16 Mbps, and 20 Mbps local area networks?

_____

_____

Lab Analysis

1. What happens to network communication when a single computer on a bus topology network fails?

    _____

    _____

2. Explain the physical design of a star bus topology and the advantage of this topology.

    _____

    _____

3. What is the difference between Thin Ethernet and Thick Ethernet?

    _____

    _____

4. What are the five grades and speeds of UTP cabling?

    _____

    _____

    _____

    _____

5. Which IEEE 802 subcommittees represent the Ethernet and Token Ring standards? Use the Internet to find this information and give a brief description on the network access method used for Ethernet.

    _____

    _____

Key Term Quiz

Use the following vocabulary terms to complete the sentences below. Not all of the terms will be used.

> bus topology
>
> coaxial
>
> Ethernet
>
> fiber optic
>
> mesh topology
>
> ring topology
>
> star topology
>
> unshielded twisted-pair (UTP)

1. The most common type of network cable used today is the _____ cable.

2. _____ describes a network in which all the computers connect to a central wiring point, or hub.

3. RG-8, often referred to as Thick Ethernet, is a _____ cable.

4. _____ cables transmit light for distances up to ten kilometers.

5. In a _____ network, each computer has a dedicated line connection to every other computer on the network.

Lab Wrap-Up

The topology and cable types that you choose for your network scenario affect not only the consistency of data transfer, but also the speed at which data reaches its destination.

Solutions

In this section, you'll find solutions to the lab exercises, the Lab Analysis questions, and the Key Term Quiz.

Lab 4.01 Solution

Step 1   A star topology connects client computers physically to a central location, usually a hub through which all data passes when communicating with other computers on the network. The star topology can also use a switch to connect computers on different network segments together. A switch passes data directly from the source computer to the destination computer and allows multiple conversations between computers to happen at the same time. This provides for a greater rate of data transmission. A bus network attaches all computers to a single physical cable and data passes from one computer on the segment to the next. A ring topology connects each computer on the ring directly to two computers until each of the connections form a single ring connection. Data travels around the ring until a connection is broken from one computer to the next, thus causing the ring to fail.

Step 2   If a computer or cable were to fail in a star topology network, the failure would not affect communication or transfer of data across the entire network, only across the affected cable and the failed computer. This is an advantage over a bus or ring topology. If the cabling fails in either a bus or ring topology, the transfer of data halts until the break is repaired.

Step 3   A star bus topology and star ring topology are two hybrid solutions that Prayias International may consider. A star bus topology provides a physical star topology with a logical bus. The client's computers connect to a central hub, which takes the incoming data from one cable and passes it to the other nodes on the network. The clients act as if they are connected on a bus network, yet if one of them fails, the others are not affected. A star ring network is a hybrid topology that encompasses both the star and ring topologies. The physical topology is designed as a star, with all computers plugging into a central hub, wherein the logical ring topology is hidden and applied. The communication between clients relies on both the logical and physical aspects of the network.

Step 4   Prayias International should implement either the ring or star bus topology, which provides for the highest level of fault tolerance. Fault tolerance is the ability of a system to continue functioning even when some part of the system has failed, thus denying what's known as a "single point of failure," in which even one failed device or cable causes the entire network to fail. Both the ring and star bus methods provide fault tolerance. These hybrid topologies are common in today's networks and can be implemented in all office locations for Prayias International.

Lab 4.02 Solution

Step 1   Answers will vary, but can include RG-58 coaxial cable (Thin Ethernet), UTP, STP, and fiber optic.

Step 2   The RG-58 coaxial cable appears rounded, similar to the type of cable used for cable television. It may have a connector on each end that resembles a barrel or the letter T. The Ohm rating, a relative measure of the resistance on the cable, should appear as a marking on the cable. The Ohm rating for the RG-58 coaxial cable is 50 Ohm. A television cable, though similar in appearance, has a 75 Ohm value. The RG-58 cable requires a 50 Ohm terminator on each end of the cable in a bus topology network to prevent the signal from traveling back and forth across the network, hindering communication. The UTP cable will be flat and thin in appearance with connectors at each end that appear similar to connectors used on telephone cables. Fiber optic cables appear to be made of rounded plastic; however, they possess a central glass or plastic core. Their connectors may appear to have inner cables extended through their rounded, barrel shapes.

Step 3   Answers will vary, but can include category markings for UTP cables written on the cables' outer shells. Categories may include Category 1–5(e).

Step 4   Answers will vary for cable type. UTP categories include

- Category 1—no data communication

- Category 2—4 Mbps

- Category 3—16 Mbps

- Category 4—20 Mbps

- Category 5(e)—100 Mbps

Step 5   Speeds of 100 Mbps can be accommodated by two different cabling options. UTP Category 5 cables can support speeds up to 100 Mbps over 100-meter segments, and fiber optic cables can support speeds of 100 Mbps over 2000-meter segments. If Greening Antiques' network does not reach the 100 Mbps optimum bandwidth, some possible factors that may be responsible for the slowdown in throughput include too many users on a single network segment, high demand from networked applications, such as e-mail with large attached files, and high demand from desktop publishing and multimedia bandwidth-intensive applications.

Step 6   Greening Antiques requires an inexpensive cabling solution for their network; therefore, the appropriate choice would be UTP Category 5 cabling. This cabling supports the data transfer rates at a lower cost than fiber optic cabling.

Lab 4.03 Solution

Step 1   The design should encompass several servers connected directly to a single dedicated backbone (bus) connection. The design should also indicate two segments connected to the backbone that contain multiple computers connected to one another in a mesh topology. Both segments should show the mesh topology between workstation computers, while servers should remain directly connected to the backbone, separate from the mesh topology.

Step 2   Mesh topology can sometimes be messy, as every computer on a segment must connect to every other computer directly, resulting in much cabling and in some cases, multiple NICs adding to the expense. Though this topology provides fault tolerance, it is not effective in real life and you can replace it in this scenario with a star bus topology for each location's segment of workstation computers. These segments would remain connected directly to the Ethernet backbone, enabling communication and data transfer between segments in the various cities. This scenario has the advantage of a cleaner design (less cabling) and efficient communication.

Step 3

Restaurant Location	Minimum Data Transfer Speed	UTP Category
New York City	20 Mbps	UTP Category 4 or higher
Chicago	16 Mbps	UTP Category 3 or higher
Boston	10 Mbps	UTP Category 3 or higher
Montreal	100 Mbps	UTP Category 5
New Orleans	4 Mbps	UTP Category 2 or higher

Step 4   There is no need to change the backbone infrastructure to effectively change the topology of the current network segments to enable efficient data communication. The star bus topology suggestion will not affect the current backbone infrastructure and will maintain effective communication with less cabling than the previous mesh topology.

Step 5   It would be advantageous to use a Category 5 UTP cabling plant to support all of the above data rates because it is an inexpensive option that provides a high-speed transfer rate without the need for future upgrades due to overutilization.

Answers to Lab Analysis

1.   When a single computer on a bus topology network fails, the network communication halts, as this failed computer affects all other computers on the LAN. A bus topology is made up of a central bus cable that connects all computers. Data is sent across the single cable from one computer to the next computer on the cable. If that computer has failed,

the data is unable to be transferred on the network, as a break in the backbone from a single failed computer will result in a complete failure to the network.

2. In a star bus topology, all computers connect to a central hub, using a physical star design. The advantage of this topology is that a break in any cable only affects the computer connected to that particular cable. The data communication between the remainder of the network can continue without interruption.

3. Thick Ethernet (10-Base-5) uses RG-8 cabling and is an old technology that is rarely used today. The thick cable is used exclusively in Thick Ethernet networks and provides a speed of 10 Mbps. Its segments can be 500 meters in length. Thin Ethernet (10-Base-2) uses RG-58 coaxial cabling. The thin cables also provide a speed of 10 Mbps but the segments can be a maximum of 185 meters long.

4. UTP cabling categories:

   - Category 1—analog phone lines with no data communication

   - Category 2—speed of up to 4 Mbps

   - Category 3—speed of up to 16 Mbps

   - Category 4—speed of up to 20 Mbps

   - Category 5(e)—speed of up to 100 Mbps

5. The IEEE 802.3 carrier sense multiple access with collision detection (CSMA/CD) Access Method Subcommittee is also known as the Ethernet standard. The IEEE 802.5 subcommittee represents the Token Ring Access Method standard. CSMA/CD provides rules that govern how data is transferred across a network from multiple devices simultaneously. Each computer on the network checks the cable for traffic before transmitting data and only sends when the cable is free of traffic. All data must reach the destination before another device may transmit data. If a collision is detected, the transmitting device will delay retransmission on subsequent attempts.

Answers to Key Term Quiz

1. unshielded twisted-pair (UTP)

2. star topology

3. coaxial

4. fiber optic

5. mesh topology

Chapter **5**

Ethernet Basics

Lab Exercises

The industry de facto standard known as Ethernet defines and resolves many different issues involved in transferring data between computers on a network. Ethernet uses data packets that contain MAC addresses to determine the sending and receiving of data through the use of the carrier sense multiple access with collision detection (CSMA/CD) protocol. These labs will help you understand the Ethernet technology and the various cabling specifications and hardware devices that enhance data delivery across an Ethernet network.

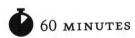 60 MINUTES

Lab 5.01: Examining Ethernet Technology

The company that you work for is considering implementing an Ethernet network. Your boss has asked you to present the advantages and capabilities of this technology to help determine if this solution is optimal for the company. You must explain the function of CSMA/CD in your presentation.

Learning Objectives

In this lab, you'll examine the concept and process of the Ethernet technology. At the end of this lab, you will be able to

- Describe the capabilities and advantages of an Ethernet network

- Define the function of CSMA/CD

- Illustrate the purpose of terminating resistors

Lab Materials and Setup

For this lab exercise, you'll need

- Pencil and paper

- Internet access

Getting Down to Business

Step 1   To format your presentation, you must determine how Ethernet organizes and transmits data. In the following space, provide a brief description of this process. If necessary, use the Internet to help with your research.

_____

_____

Step 2   Define the function and advantages of the CSMA/CD protocol.

_____

_____

Step 3   Explain the concept of termination through the use of terminating resistors as shown in Figure 5-1.

_____

_____

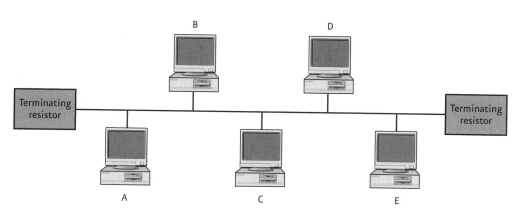

FIGURE 5-1 Terminating resistors on a bus cable

 45 MINUTES

Lab 5.02: Analyzing Ethernet Cabling Specifications

You are trying to set up your home network and you want to adhere to the IEEE 802.3 standard for cabling. You are implementing a very small network of five client computers and one server as shown in Figure 5-2. You must determine what cable specifications will meet your needs. Your cable options include the 10-Base-2 and 10-Base-5 standard cable types.

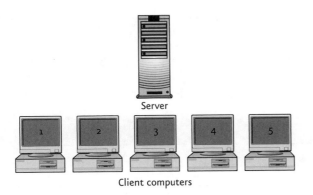

FIGURE 5-2 Small home network

Learning Objectives

In this lab, you'll examine the process of setting up a home network using Ethernet cabling. At the end of this lab, you will be able to

- Define the Ethernet 10-Base-2 and 10-Base-5 cabling standards

- Design a small home network

Lab Materials and Setup

For this lab exercise, you'll need

- Pencil and paper

- Internet access

Getting Down to Business

Step 1   List the Ethernet cable specifications in the following table.

Standard	Cable Type	Connection Type	Maximum Length	Maximum Speed
10-Base-2	_____	_____	_____	_____
10-Base-5	_____	_____	_____	_____

Step 2   List the hardware necessary to establish a home network that would adhere to your desires. Limit your cabling options to the 10-Base-2 and 10-Base-5 standards.

_____

_____

✔ **Hint**

Keep in mind the cabling options and computer hardware necessary to network clients and servers on an Ethernet network.

Step 3   Would repeaters or bridges be necessary in this home network? Why or why not?

_____

_____

 45 MINUTES

Lab 5.03: Comparing Hardware Devices on an Ethernet Network

Steffen Network Solutions has hired you to work in their sales department where you will specialize in network hardware. Your first client, a fast-growing research company, has asked you to recommend a hardware solution for their environment. They currently implement a Thick Ethernet network using 10-Base-5 RG-8 cabling in their single office. They are expanding to create another office on a separate floor in an office building approximately 700 meters away and wish to have both offices able to communicate on the same LAN. The research company also requires the ability to filter traffic on the network, preserving bandwidth.

Learning Objectives

In this lab, you'll compare bridges and repeaters on an Ethernet network and make a hardware recommendation for a network environment. At the end of this lab, you will be able to

- Define and compare bridges and repeaters
- Recommend a hardware solution for a company network

Lab Materials and Setup

For this lab exercise, you'll need

- Pencil and paper
- Internet access

Getting Down to Business

Step 1   In the following space, describe the function of a repeater and the advantages of implementing one on an Ethernet network.

Step 2   In the following space, describe the function of a bridge and the advantages of implementing one on an Ethernet network.

_____

_____

Step 3   Suggest a hardware solution for the research company using either repeaters, bridges, or both. Research the Internet for information that will assist you in making a recommendation.

_____

_____

Step 4   How does your recommended hardware solution provide advantages for the cabling that the company is currently implementing?

_____

_____

Lab Analysis

1. How does the MAC address determine whether the packet being delivered across an Ethernet wire is for the computer that possesses this physical address defined in the packet?

_____

_____

2. What would happen to communication if a cable break were to occur between a single computer on a bus cable and the rest of the computers attached to the wire in an Ethernet network?

_____

_____

3. What are the limitations of 10-Base-5 cabling and why is it not often used in today's network environments?

_____

_____

4. Compare the Baseband signaling method used on Ethernet networks and the Broadband signaling method used by cable modems and cable television.

_____

_____

5. What is the main feature that a bridge offers an Ethernet network that a repeater does not provide?

_____

_____

Key Term Quiz

Use the following vocabulary terms to complete the sentences below. Not all of the terms will be used.

Baseband

binary code

BNC connector

bridge

Broadband

CSMA/CD

packet

packet sniffer

repeater

T connector

transceivers

1. A _____ is a device that takes packets from one segment and retransmits them on another Ethernet segment.

2. _____ sends a simple single data signal over a network cable.

3. The _____ transmit and receive signals on cables between computer hardware.

4. A 10-Base-2 NIC connects to the bus cable using a _____.

5. A system called _____ determines which computers can use a shared cable at any given time to send data.

Lab Wrap-Up

The Ethernet standard deals with many different issues involved in transferring data between computers on a network. You have seen how the cabling, hardware, signaling type, and CSMA/CD protocol used in the Ethernet network can affect the transmission of data. The next chapter will introduce the 10-Base-T modern Ethernet standard.

Solutions

In this section, you'll find solutions to the lab exercises, the Lab Analysis questions, and the Key Term Quiz.

Lab 5.01 Solution

Step 1   A computer on an Ethernet network transmits Baseband signals one bit at a time over the network cable. An Ethernet LAN most often uses coaxial or twisted-pair cables. A computer listens to the channel, and when the channel is idle, it transmits an Ethernet frame. This frame contains the MAC address of the source and recipient and a CRC code. All other computers connected to the cable listen to see if the frame is meant for them, containing their unique MAC address. If the computer finds a frame with its MAC address, it opens the frame and processes the data.

Step 2   The carrier sense multiple access with collision detection (CSMA/CD) protocol is used on an Ethernet network to determine which computer on the network shared cable should be allowed to send data across the wire at a given time. Each node on the network must wait until the network is free of any signals, called carriers, before it can begin to transmit data across the cable. This process is called carrier sense. Multiple access means that all computers are equal in their ability to send data on the network. No one computer has priority over any another computer. Collision detection is the process of listening for occasional signals on the network that may collide, preventing this collision by stopping the transmission and sending the data at a later time. All of these features of CSMA/CD combine to produce the advantage of sending data across a network cable with multiple access and collision detection.

Step 3   When electrical signals travel to the end of copper wires, some of the energy reflects and travels back up the wire. These reflections prevent the other computers from sending data across the wire, and the network appears to be permanently busy. To prevent these reflective signals, termination must occur. Terminating resistors can be connected to the ends of segments to absorb the reflections. Once the signals are absorbed, the segment will function normally and the wire will appear free from busy signals. These terminating resistors must attach to the end of Ethernet cables. The Ohmic value of these terminating resistors is 50 Ohms. It is important to note the Ohmic value of the terminating resistor, as other values are present such as 75 Ohms. 50 Ohms is the value for terminating on an Ethernet bus.

Lab 5.02 Solution

Step 1

Standard	Cable Type	Connection Type	Maximum Length	Maximum Speed
10-Base-2	RG-58 Thinnet coaxial	BNC, T connector	185 meters	10 Mbps
10-Base-5	RG-8 Thicknet coaxial	AUI connector	500 meters	10 Mbps

Step 2 Establishing a home network with five client computers and one server requires that each computer have an NIC installed. The 10-Base-2 and 10-Base-5 cable options available for a small home network include RG-58 and RG-8 coaxial. Thick Ethernet (10-Base-5) is rarely used today. Thin Ethernet (10-Base-2) provides a speed of 10 Mbps and segments can be a maximum of 185 meters long, providing both distance and adequate speed for a small home network. 10-Base-T UTP Categories 3, 4, and 5 also provide distances of 100 meters.

Step 3 Repeaters and bridges are not necessary in a small network if the overall distance of the network is satisfied with one network segment. Repeaters retransmit data over multiple network segments and bridges transmit data to multiple segments as well as filter data traffic. Only if you are segmenting your network should you consider implementing either a repeater or bridge.

Lab 5.03 Solution

Step 1 A repeater is a hardware device that takes all data packets on one segment and retransmits them on another network segment. The advantages of using a repeater on an Ethernet network are that a repeater can extend the distance of the network, provide support for additional computers to connect to the network, provide fault tolerance if cable breaks occur on a limited segment, and link various types of cable segments together.

Step 2 A bridge is a hardware device that filters and forwards traffic between two LANs or two network segments on the same LAN based on the MAC addresses contained in the data packets. They are protocol independent and can be either a stand-alone device or a computer with two NICs running bridge software. The advantage of using a bridge is that it provides improved performance by segmenting the network traffic. A bridge also detects any collisions that may occur and is responsible for retransmitting packets.

Step 3   The research company requires a hardware solution that will fit with their 10-Base-5 Ethernet network that implements RG-8 cables, and that will provide the ability to segment network traffic. Bridges will provide an optimal solution for this network as they provide filtering of network traffic and extend the distance that the network can cover by adding segments, as 10-Base-5 segments cannot be longer than 500 meters. Repeaters would extend the distance of the network, but they do not provide filtering. If two computers on different network segments (that are connected by a repeater) send packets at the same time, a collision will result. Bridges provide filtering between collision domains (Ethernet segments).

Step 4   Because the distance restrictions on the 10-Base-5 RG-8 cables indicate that each cable may not be longer than 500 meters, the addition of a bridge will allow for an extended LAN in terms of total distance, without limiting the performance of the network due to traffic jams caused by collisions.

Answers to Lab Analysis

1. Each MAC address is a unique 48-bit binary address, also written in hexadecimal notation. If the unique MAC address that exists on the NIC of the receiving computer is identical to the destination MAC address defined in the packet, the computer will attempt to receive the packet and process the data. All other computers on the network that have different physical addresses will not attempt to accept the packet for processing.

2. If a cable break were to occur between one computer and the rest of the network, that computer would not be able to communicate with the rest of the network. Also, because the cable break affects the terminated ends of the bus cable, the signal will now reflect back over the wire, cause all computers on the network to suspend attempted delivery of data, and shut down the network.

3. The 10-Base-5 cabling (RG-8), running at 10 Mbps, is not often used in today's network environments because it has several disadvantages. The cost of this cabling is expensive compared to that of other cabling systems, and it is also more difficult to install. The RG-8 cable is extremely stiff and the AUI connectors are more difficult to install and support than BNC connectors used with 10-Base-2 cabling.

4. Baseband signaling sends a single signal over the cable. Broadband signaling takes multiple signals and creates a unique channel for each signal frequency. Baseband signaling is currently used almost exclusively on Ethernet networks; however this may change in the future due to the increased use of cable modems to connect to the Internet, which use Broadband signaling.

5. A bridge offers the ability to filter network traffic in a LAN or network segment based on MAC addresses. Both the repeater and bridge extend the distance of a network through the use of segments; however, the repeater does not manage traffic, it only repeats the data signals or retransmits them on multiple segments.

Answers to Key Term Quiz

1. repeater
2. Baseband
3. transceivers
4. BNC connector
5. CSMA/CD

Chapter 6
Modern Ethernet

Lab Exercises

The introduction of modern Ethernet standards has enabled companies around the world to build large, flexible, fast networks. Where older Ethernet networks transmitted data at 10 Mbps, modern Ethernet networks can operate at 100 or even 1000 Mbps. Twisted-pair wiring and/or fiber optic wiring has replaced the older coaxial cable in many of the hybrid topologies installed throughout the industry. Hybrid topologies are a mixture of bus, star, and mesh topologies. These labs will enable you to compare Ethernet environments. You will also design network solutions for small business environments.

 30 MINUTES

Lab 6.01: Examining 10-Base-T Networks

Mainwaring & Associates, a small law firm in Melbourne, Australia, is considering changing their current 10-Base-2 network to a 10-Base-T design. They need to know the differences in the designs of both networks, the additional hardware that would need to be purchased to implement a 10-Base-T design, and the limitations of the 10-Base-T network design. They have hired you as a consultant to provide them with the answers to their questions. Mainwaring & Associates' current network design is shown in Figure 6-1.

Learning Objectives

In this lab, you'll examine the capabilities and limitations of 10-Base-T networks. At the end of this lab, you will be able to

- Compare 10-Base-T networks to 10-Base-2 and 10-Base-5 networks

- Analyze 10-Base-T network hardware specifications/requirements

- Understand the limitations of a 10-Base-T network

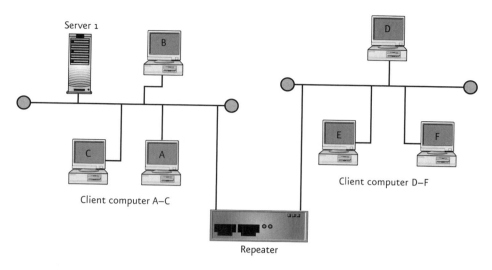

FIGURE 6-1 Mainwaring & Associates' 10-Base-2 network

Lab Materials and Setup

For this lab exercise, you'll need

- Pencil and paper

- Internet access

- 10-Base-T Ethernet hub and/or switch

- Two UTP cables with RJ-45 connectors on both ends; minimum of three feet in length

- Two working computers with 10-Base-T functional NICs installed

Getting Down to Business

Step 1   Examine and describe the Ethernet hardware in your possession. How do the 10-Base-T UTP cables differ from the coaxial cables?

Step 2   Describe the 10-Base-T topology that will be used with Ethernet hubs and/or switches and UTP cabling. How does this compare to the 10-Base-2 and 10-Base-5 network topologies?

_____

_____

Step 3   What additional hardware would Mainwaring & Associates need to purchase to upgrade from a 10-Base-2 network to a 10-Base-T network?

_____

_____

Step 4   Research on the Internet to find the limitations of a 10-Base-T network and list them in the space provided here.

_____

_____

Step 5   Connect the UTP cables to the computers and hub/switch. Ensure that your hub/switch is connected to the Internet. Ensure that all devices are in working order and that you can browse the network from both computers before you proceed.

a)   What would happen to communication if a connection to the hub/switch were to break? Disconnect one UTP cable from the hub and attempt to browse the Internet from the other computer that was not disconnected. Report your results in the space below.

_____

_____

b)   What would happen to communication if the segment inside the hub (the circuit board) were to fail? Disable the hub by powering off the device completely and attempt to browse the Internet from each computer. Report your results in the space below.

_____

_____

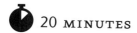 20 MINUTES

Lab 6.02: Designing an Ethernet Collision Domain

Vaughan Road Collegiate, a local high school, has hired you to design their network. The high school would like to have several departmental computers included in the network design. The following table indicates the number of computers per department.

Department	Computers
Administration	Six Windows 98 computers, two Windows NT 4.0 servers
Library	Five Windows NT Workstation 4.0 computers
Science	Ten Linux computers
Computer Science	Five Windows 95 computers

Vaughan Road Collegiate technical staff personnel are concerned about the hardware and size limitations of an Ethernet collision domain and would like you to present them with a graphical design for their network before implementing any physical changes.

Learning Objectives

In this lab, you'll design an Ethernet collision domain. At the end of this lab, you will be able to

- Define the 5-4-3 rule used in 10-Base-T networks
- Draw a design of a small Ethernet collision domain network

Lab Materials and Setup

For this lab exercise, you'll need

- Pencil and paper
- Internet access

Getting Down to Business

Step 1   Briefly describe the set of restrictions known as the 5-4-3 rule in the space provided here. Use the Internet to assist you in your research and list a minimum of three web sites where you obtain your results.

Step 2   What additional hardware must be present in your network design for Vaughan Road Collegiate, aside from the computers already present on their network? List the hardware in the space provided below. Research the Internet to find a minimum of three web sites for companies in your city that sell the hardware that you need. Record these web sites for future use.

Step 3   On a separate piece of paper, draw a network design that will satisfy the requirements of Vaughan Road Collegiate.

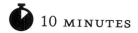 10 MINUTES

Lab 6.03: Analyzing High-Speed Ethernet Options

Balmer Technology Solutions, a networking solutions company, has recently hired you. They have asked you to research the current high-speed Ethernet solutions available today and present your findings at the upcoming company conference.

Learning Objectives

In this lab, you'll analyze high-speed Ethernet options for today's network environments. At the end of this lab, you will be able to

- Match the technology with the desired features and capabilities of a high-speed Ethernet solution

- Identify the clear advantages and disadvantages of 100 Mbps and 1000 Mbps Ethernet over existing 10 Mbps Ethernet environments

Lab Materials and Setup

For this lab exercise, you'll need

- Pencil and paper

- Internet access

Getting Down to Business

Step 1   Using the following chart, match the technology on the left with the capability on the right that it provides. Use the Internet to research each technology, if necessary.

1) 100-Base-FX   a) Uses single-mode cables for distances up to five kilometers

2) Full-Duplex   b) Similar to 10-Base-FL with maximum cable length of 400 meters

3) 1000-Base-SX   c) Uses twinaxial cable; not common in today's Ethernet market

4) 100-Base-T   d) Devices can send and receive data simultaneously

5) 1000-Base-LX   e) Uses fiber optic cabling and SC connectors and 500-meter maximum cable lengths

6) 1000-Base-CX   f) Uses star bus topology and 100-meter cable maximum distance

Lab Analysis

1. When upgrading from a current 10-Base-2 environment to a 10-Base-T environment, would any of the existing hardware be utilized in the new 10-Base-T solution?

    _____

    _____

2. What is 10-Base-FL? How does it differ from 10-Base-T? List the advantages of 10-Base-FL over the 10-Base-T cabling.

    _____

    _____

3. What IEEE standards are registered for Gigabit Ethernet? List the advantages and disadvantages of standard Gigabit Ethernet.

    _____

    _____

4. What is the purpose of having a maximum size for an Ethernet collision domain?

    _____

    _____

5. How is full-duplex mode implemented in Ethernet networks?

    _____

    _____

Key Term Quiz

Use the following vocabulary terms to complete the sentences below. Not all of the terms will be used.

10-Base-FL

10-Base-T

100-Base-T

crossover cable

fast Ethernet

full-duplex

RJ-45

single point of failure

star bus topology

UTP cable

1. A _____ is a special twisted-pair cable that can connect hubs together.

2. Although similar to 10-Base-2 and 10-Base-5, _____ differs due to the location of its Ethernet segment that lies protected inside a hub.

3. The _____ connector contains eight pins and is used by UTP cabling.

4. A _____ device is one that can send and receive data simultaneously.

5. _____ refers to several Ethernet technologies that operate at 100 Mbps.

Lab Wrap-Up

The use of UTP and fiber optic Ethernet networks provides for the fast, reliable, and flexible networks we see in today's corporate world. The use of switches, hubs, and high-speed cables enables network communication to flourish and networks to increase in scalability. In the next chapter, we will look at non-Ethernet standards implemented in today's networks.

Solutions

In this section, you'll find solutions to the lab exercises, the Lab Analysis questions, and the Key Term Quiz.

Lab 6.01 Solution

Step 1   The 10-Base-T UTP cables use RJ-45 8-pin connectors that resemble the RJ-11 connectors used on telephone cables. The UTP cables are flat cables and have four pairs of wires, each wire connecting to a pin on the 8-pin connector. 10-Base-2 coaxial cables use either BNC or T-connectors and are rounded cables, similar in appearance to television cable. Both cables transmit at speeds of up to 10 Mbps and use Baseband signals. The UTP cables transmit for distances up to 100 meters between the hub and the node, while the 10-Base-2 cables transmit over distances up to 185 meters/segment.

Step 2   The physical topology that is implemented with a 10-Base-T network is known as the star bus topology—using a physical star and logical bus design. The 10-Base-2 and 10-Base-5 networks both implement a standard bus topology.

Step 3   For Mainwaring & Associates to upgrade to a 10-Base-T network environment, they would have to purchase at least one 10-Base-T Ethernet hub and/or switch. The physical topology requires that all computers on the network connect to a central hub and/or switch in a 10-Base-T Ethernet network. Hubs and/or switches are not necessary in a 10-Base-2 network design, as they implement a bus topology.

Step 4   A 10-Base-T system has a distance limitation of 100 meters for the twisted-pair cable connecting a computer to a hub. The 10-Base-T network may also not have more than 1024 computers connected to the hub. Refer to the *Network+ All-in-One Certification Exam Guide, Second Edition* for additional detailed information on network size limitations.

Step 5   Disconnecting a single UTP cable from the hub will simply disable the communication between the computer that it was attached to and the rest of the network.

   a)   Disconnecting a single UTP cable from the hub will simply disable the communication between the computer that it was attached to and the rest of the network.

   b)   Disabling the hub will affect all communication on the network segment. All computers that are connected to the hub, via UTP cables, will no longer be able to communicate with each other or to the Internet.

Lab 6.02 Solution

Step 1   The 5-4-3 rule defines the maximum size of an Ethernet collision domain. The 5-4-3 rule states that in an Ethernet collision domain, no two computers may be separated by more than 5 segments, 4 repeaters, and 3 populated segments. Hubs and/or switches can be counted as both repeaters and segments when calculating the size of the entire network. A populated segment is defined as a segment that has one or more computers attached directly to it.

Step 2   To implement a 10-Base-T network, Vaughan Road Collegiate will have to acquire several additional pieces of hardware. They will have to acquire UTP cabling for all computers, NICs (if needed), several hubs and/or switches, and several crossover or coaxial cables to attach the hubs together to enable communication between network segments. Web sites that provide sales of these hardware items will vary based on city.

Step 3   Figure 6-2 shows a network design that will satisfy the requirements of Vaughan Road Collegiate.

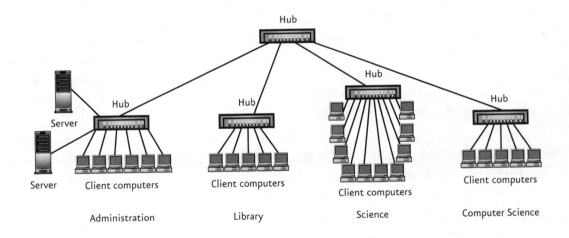

FIGURE 6-2 Vaughan Road Collegiate's 10-Base-T network

Lab 6.03 Solution

Step 1   Answers: 1-b; 2-d; 3-e; 4-f; 5-a; 6-c.

Answers to Lab Analysis

1. In addition to the computers with 10-Base-T NICs, a 10-Base-T network requires a minimum of one UTP cable with an RJ-45 connector on each end per computer, and an Ethernet hub. There would be no existing hardware that would be utilized in the new 10-Base-T solution.

2. 10-Base-FL is a fiber optic version of the 10-Base-T standard that supports cables of up to 2 kilometers in length with SC or ST connectors. 10-Base-T UTP cables with RJ-45 connectors support cable lengths of only 100 meters from the hub to a computer. 10-Base-FL uses light pulses to transmit data so the cables are immune to electrical interference. This cabling is also more secure than 10-Base-T UTP cables, which can be tapped into more easily.

3. Gigabit Ethernet represents the common standards 1000-Base-T, 1000-Base-CX, 1000-Base-SX, and 1000-Base-LX. Gigabit Ethernet provides the fastest speeds available in networks and, depending on the standard used, can send data over distances of up to 70 kilometers with the use of repeaters. A disadvantage of Gigabit Ethernet is the higher expense, compared to other technologies.

4. The purpose of having a maximum size for an Ethernet collision domain is to prevent undetected collisions that may occur on large networks. If the last byte sent by a computer is sent before the first byte of the packet sent reaches all computers on the network, then it may collide with other data packets, due to the fact that computers on the network do not check for collisions once the last byte of data is sent.

5. Full-duplex is implemented through the use of Ethernet switches. A switched Ethernet connection uses separate wires for sending and receiving, enabling full-duplex mode for all attached NICs that support full-duplex mode.

Answers to Key Term Quiz

1. crossover cable

2. 10-Base-T

3. RJ-45

4. full-duplex

5. fast Ethernet

Chapter 7

Non-Ethernet Networks

Lab Exercises

Though Ethernet networks seem to be the most common in today's business environments, there are many other technologies available for implementation. After Ethernet, Token Ring is the most frequently used technology today. In this chapter, we will examine the Token Ring network technology and also compare some technologies of the past. ARCNet (Attached Resource Computer Network) and LocalTalk are examples of past technologies, while Fiber Distributed Data Interface (FDDI) and Asynchronous Transfer Mode (ATM), two high-speed networking standards, exist today, though not in any great measure.

 15 MINUTES

Lab 7.01: Understanding Token Ring Networks

Nixon-Craig University has implemented a Token Ring network that they have hired you to support. The network consists of several 4/16 Mbps Token Ring nodes and several 4 Mbps Token Ring nodes. The network has implemented a physical star topology with multiple Multistation Access Units (MAUs) and nodes connected via UTP cabling. The users on the network are complaining of a slow network. Based on your knowledge of Token Ring networks, you know that data is normally transmitted without delay.

Learning Objectives

In this lab, you'll examine Token Ring networks. At the end of this lab, you will be able to

- Describe how Token Ring networks operate

- Identify Token Ring cabling and devices

- Resolve a Token Ring network bandwidth problem

Lab Materials and Setup

For this lab exercise, you'll need

- Pencil and paper
- Internet access

Getting Down to Business

Step 1 Based on your knowledge of Token Ring networks, explain the process of data delivery and how available bandwidth is utilized through token passing.

_____

_____

Step 2 What hardware devices and cabling options are available for use in a Token Ring network? List them in the spaces provided here. How does the implementation of each cabling option affect the physical layout of the Token Ring network?

_____

_____

Step 3 Based on the Nixon-Craig University network environment described in the Lab 7.01 case study, what is the probable cause of the slow bandwidth? Can this problem be resolved, and if so, how?

_____

_____

20 MINUTES

Lab 7.02: Comparing Non-Ethernet Networks

Your company has sent you to a remote location in northern Canada where you discover two network technologies being implemented that you have not seen in recent years. Gleason Mines, a small zinc mining company, has implemented both an ARCNet network and a LocalTalk network within their physical environment. You are not familiar with the features of these older technologies and before attempting to administer each network, you decide to research their histories thoroughly.

Learning Objectives

In this lab, you'll compare several non-Ethernet networks. At the end of this lab, you will be able to

- Recognize ARCNet and LocalTalk network environments
- Compare FDDI and ATM technologies by listing the advantages and disadvantages of both

Lab Materials and Setup

For this lab exercise, you'll need

- Pencil and paper
- Internet access

Getting Down to Business

Step 1   Using the Internet, research the ARCNet and LocalTalk network technologies and indicate their histories in the space provided.

Step 2 Additional non-Ethernet network technologies appeared over the last several decades. FDDI and ATM are examples of these technologies. Compare and list the main features of each technology in the space provided here. Give a brief list of the advantages and disadvantages of each.

Lab Analysis

1. Why does the Token Ring network technology use a physical star topology rather than a physical ring topology?

   _____

   _____

2. How are multiple Multistation Access Units (MAUs) connected in a Token Ring network?

   _____

   _____

3. Indicate two reasons why Token Ring networks are not as predominant in the industry as Ethernet networks.

   _____

   _____

4. Token passing is a deterministic method of determining access to the network wire. Define the term _deterministic_ as it relates to token passing.

   _____

   _____

5. What was the predominant reason for the introduction of the FDDI and ATM technologies?

   _____

   _____

Key Term Quiz

Use the following vocabulary terms to complete the sentences below. Not all of the terms will be used.

active hub

Copper Data Distribution Interface (CDDI)

cyclical redundancy check (CRC)

Fiber Distributed Data Interface (FDDI)

Frame Check Sequence (FCS)

IEEE 802.4

IEEE 802.5

logical ring

Multistation Access Unit (MAU)

Network Address Translation (NAT)

passive hub

physical ring

token passing

1. A _____ is part of a Token Ring that is used to check for data errors.

2. ARCNet technology is popular in small networks and can use a basic hub, also known as a _____.

3. The _____ committee defines the standards for Token Ring.

4. A Token Ring hub is also known as a _____.

5. _____ is a standard that provides the features of a firewall by hiding internal IP addresses.

Lab Wrap-Up

As you have seen, there are several network technologies that have existed and still do exist aside from the ever-popular Ethernet technology. The most recent technology that is currently growing in popularity is the wireless network technology. Based on the increase in both the speeds and sizes of networks over the years, the future of wireless network technologies looks promising. Networks require speed, reliability, scalability, expandability, and affordability to meet today's business requirements. The constant is change. Considering these requirements, it is obvious to most casual observers that there are several evolving technical solutions to meet these demands. Ethernet is the most pervasive de facto Media Access Control (MAC) protocol in the industry today, but it is not the *only* solution. There are many other types of methods used to control the flow of data on a local area network; however, the price tag can become a restrictive factor when considering the implementation of newer technologies. To keep abreast of current and future technologies requires IT professionals to be constantly informed of changing technologies and how they may impact existing systems in place today. To accomplish this, technicians should be well read using various periodicals and the Internet to make the best decision based on the tools that are available in the market today and their future in tomorrow's world of networking. One such periodical that has achieved notoriety is *Network Computing*. You are encouraged to visit their web site at www.networkcomputing.com to see where the industry is today and where it may be tomorrow. To quote Sir Francis Bacon (1561–1626), "Nam et ipsa scientia potestas est," which means, "Knowledge is power!"

Solutions

In this section, you'll find solutions to the lab exercises, the Lab Analysis questions, and the Key Term Quiz.

Lab 7.01 Solution

Step 1   Unlike Ethernet, which is a contention-based method of controlling the flow of data on the wire, Token Ring networks employ a token-passing system to control access to the logical ring topology of the network using a contentionless method. Ethernet uses a contention-based method called CSMA/CD (carrier sense multiple access with collision detection), whereas Token Ring uses a contentionless method known as CSMA/CA (carrier sense multiple access with collision avoidance).

Token passing simply means that a computer is only allowed to transmit data on the network when it possesses a special packet called the token that is passed around the ring. Computers on a Token Ring network can only communicate directly with two other computers: one that provides an upstream communication and one that receives the downstream communication in the ring. Once a computer possesses the token, it can send data across the network, passing directly to its downstream neighbor computer, and across the network to the final destination computer receiving the data packet. Token passing allows more than one computer to send data at any given time. This feature allows for minimal wasted bandwidth because there are no collisions to resolve. Each computer on the network has been allotted permission to send packets and has to abide by certain rules that govern how long a computer may retain the token. There is no random access to the wire and therefore no possible collisions to resolve.

Step 2   Token Ring networks implement a physical star topology and a logical ring topology. Because of this, all computers on a segment will need to connect to a central hub, known as a Multistation Access Unit (MAU). Token Ring networks can operate using either shielded twisted-pair (STP) or unshielded twisted-pair (UTP) cabling. Depending on which cabling type you choose to implement, the physical layout of your network may vary.

If implementing Token Ring over STP, which is uncommon in today's networks because of its expense, a single Token Ring MAU can support up to 260 computers. The length of the STP cables connecting a computer to the MAU is also restricted to 100 meters.

If implementing Token Ring over UTP (an inexpensive option), your network segments will seem much smaller. This type of Token Ring network can support up to 72 computers per MAU, and the length of the UTP cable connecting a computer to the MAU is restricted to 45 meters.

Step 3   The speed at which a Token Ring network operates is dependant on the speed of the devices on the ring. The slowest device on the ring will determine the effective speed of the network. In the case of Nixon-Craig University, because they have multiple 4 Mbps Token Ring computers, the speed of the network will be 4 Mbps. If these computers were upgraded to a faster speed, or eliminated from the network, the overall speed of the network would increase.

Lab 7.02 Solution

Step 1   The ARCNet technology was developed by the Datapoint Corporation in 1977. It is a simple and inexpensive method of connecting computers together to form a LAN. The topology of the network is a physical star. ARCNet networks can use both UTP and coaxial cabling and pass data from one computer to the next using token passing. ARCNet networks can support up to 255 computers and transmit data at a slow rate of 2.5 Mbps.

LocalTalk networks were developed by Apple Computer and are also inexpensive and easy to maintain. They use a physical bus topology with unique LocalTalk cabling and connectors. The speed of the LocalTalk network is also very slow. Its speed of transmission is only 230 Kbps.

Step 2   Fiber Distributed Data Interface (FDDI) is a high-speed technology specifically designed to run on fiber optic or UTP cables at 100 Mbps. Fiber optic cabling allows for distances of up to two kilometers in length per network segment. UTP cabling allows for a maximum distance of 100 meters. FDDI uses a unique dual-ring physical topology. Data is sent on one of the rings and if a break occurs, portions of the second ring are used to create a new complete ring to keep the data moving to its destination without failure.

ATM is a technology that sends data packets of a fixed size only. It supports speeds from 155 to 2448 Mbps and is often used to transmit audio, video, and images. It implements a physical star topology and can support both UTP and fiber optic cabling.

Answers to Lab Analysis

1. The Token Ring network uses a physical star topology over a physical ring topology because if the ring fails in a physical ring topology, the entire network will be shut down. The traffic flowing around the ring will never reach its final destination and new tokens will never be created.

2. In a Token Ring network, multiple MAUs are connected through the special ports labeled Ring In and Ring Out. The Ring In port on the first MAU must connect to the Ring Out port on the second MAU, and vice versa to form a logical ring.

3. Token Ring networks are more expensive than Ethernet networks because of the cost of the Token Ring devices. Secondly, fast Ethernet and Gigabit Ethernet networks provide faster speeds than 16 Mbps Token Ring networks.

4. *Deterministic* means that computers are granted access to the network wire in a logical, predictable way, through the possession of a token. This differs from the random Ethernet method of CSMA/CD.

5. The increase in demand for bandwidth led to the creation of the FDDI and ATM network technologies. Both technologies support speeds of at least 100 Mbps.

Answers to Key Term Quiz

1. Frame Check Sequence (FCS)

2. passive hub

3. IEEE 802.5

4. Multistation Access Unit (MAU)

5. Network Address Translation (NAT)

Chapter 8

NICs

Lab Exercises

Network interface cards (NICs) are necessary components of computers in today's network environments. NICs are expansion circuit boards that can be added to computers to provide full-time connections to the network. They enable the sending and receiving of data from computer systems in a variety of networks, such as a 10-Base-T Ethernet and Token Ring networks. In fact, NICs are specifically designed for the individual LAN transmission technology. Each NIC will also work with one or multiple cables and connectors. In this chapter, you will learn to compare NICs and install a NIC in a computer running Windows 2000.

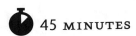 45 MINUTES

Lab 8.01: Recognizing Network Interface Cards

You wish to work as a sales technician for a small computer supply store. You are unfamiliar with all of the products currently on the market. You need to ensure that you can recognize NICs on sight to recommend and sell them to customers. To prepare for a job interview, without purchasing each individual card on the market, you choose to learn to identify the NICs from photos you have found on the Internet.

Learning Objectives

In this lab, you'll examine the types of NICs available today. At the end of this lab, you will be able to

- Identify NICs
- Compare NIC connectors

Lab Materials and Setup

For this lab exercise, you'll need

- Pencil and paper

- PC running Windows 9x and/or Windows 2000

Getting Down to Business

Step 1   Identify and label the types of NICs according to the illustrations provided in Figures 8-1 through 8-5.

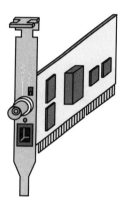

FIGURE 8-1   NIC #1

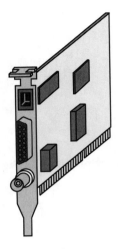

FIGURE 8-2 NIC #2

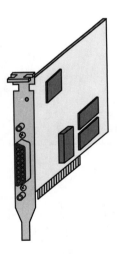

FIGURE 8-3 NIC #3

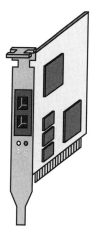

FIGURE 8-4 NIC #4

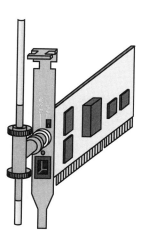

FIGURE 8-5 NIC #5

Step 2   List the visible connectors on each NIC shown in Step 1.

_____

_____

_____

_____

_____

Step 3   What networks typically use combo cards? Why?

_____

_____

Step 4   What connectors are typically used by the following NICs:

  a)   10-Base-2

_____

_____

  b)   10-Base-T

_____

_____

  c)   10-Base-FX

_____

_____

  d)   Token Ring

_____

_____

 45 MINUTES

Lab 8.02: Installing an Ethernet NIC

A call center has hired you as a technical support specialist. Your first job is to install NICs in 40 computers. You must first verify that you have the appropriate hardware and tools to accomplish the job. You must then install the NICs and verify that they are operational.

Learning Objectives

In this lab, you'll install an Ethernet NIC in a computer. At the end of this lab, you will be able to

- Physically install a NIC

- Verify the NIC is operational

Lab Materials and Setup

For this lab exercise, you'll need

- Pencil and paper

- A motherboard with a PCI bus and PnP-compatible BIOS

- A screwdriver

- An available PCI slot

- A PnP-compatible Windows 2000 operating system

- A PnP Ethernet NIC

- A CD or floppy disk containing the drivers for the NIC

- A UTP cable with RJ-45 connector

Getting Down to Business

Step 1   Turn off your PC.

Step 2   Unscrew the case, if necessary, of your PC and install the NIC in the available PCI slot.

Step 3   Plug the UTP cable into the NIC and into your network.

Step 4   Turn on your PC and boot the Windows 2000 operating system. Windows will detect the NIC and will install the appropriate drivers (or will prompt you to insert the disk containing the drivers if PnP does not recognize the NIC).

✔ **Tech Note**

If you wish to install a NIC in a computer with a Linux operating system, you may have to do some extra configuration, as Linux is not a PnP-compatible operating system. For information on Linux, refer to www.linuxdoc.org/HOWTO/Plug-and-Play-HOWTO.html.

Step 5 When Windows 2000 finishes the installation, you will be prompted to restart the PC.

Step 6 From the Windows desktop, navigate to the Control Panel. Double-click the System icon. Select the Hardware tab, and click the Device Manager button.

Step 7 Expand Network Adapters. Double-click the network adapter that appears.

Step 8 The Windows dialog box should pop up stating that your card is working properly.

Lab Analysis

1. How can you tell if your NIC is operational by simply viewing the card after it is installed?

    _____

    _____

2. You have a NIC with an RJ-45 connector. Can you determine by only viewing the RJ-45 connector whether it is an Ethernet or Token Ring card?

    _____

    _____

3. What other methods of connecting PCs are available if NICs are not an option?

    _____

    _____

4. DB connectors are often used in today's networks. Which DB connectors are typically found in today's network environments?

    _____

    _____

5. What additional connector is available for fiber optic networks aside from the SC and ST connectors?

    _____

    _____

Key Term Quiz

Use the following vocabulary terms to complete the sentences below. Not all of the terms will be used.

auto-sensing NICs

BNC connectors

Centronics connectors

combo card

DB-15 connectors

DIX connectors

multi-speed NICs

null modem cable

RJ-45 connectors

1. A _____ is used to connect two PCs through their serial ports.

2. _____ come in both female and male versions and are the D-shaped connectors on the back of printers.

3. 10-Base-T networks use UTP cabling and _____.

4. NICs that adjust themselves to the speed of the network without any configuration are known as _____.

5. An Ethernet _____ would have both an RJ-45 and BNC connector.

Lab Wrap-Up

Congratulations! You have successfully recognized, installed, and configured a NIC, completing an essential step in ensuring that a computer can communicate on the LAN.

Solutions

In this section, you'll find solutions to the lab exercises, the Lab Analysis questions, and the Key Term Quiz.

Lab 8.01 Solution

Step 1   The NICs in Figures 8-1 through 8-5 are

NIC #1: Typical Ethernet combo card (two-way)

NIC #2: Ethernet three-way combo card

NIC #3: 10-Base-5 card

NIC #4: Fiber-optic NIC

NIC #5: 10-Base-2 NIC

Step 2   The connectors on the associated NICs are

NIC #1: BNC and RJ-45 connector

NIC #2: BNC, 15-pin DB (DIX), RJ-45 connector

NIC #3: Female 15-pin DB connector (DIX)

NIC #4: SC connectors

NIC #5: RJ-45, BNC, and T-connector

Step 3   Combo cards are typically used for Ethernet NICs, as Ethernet networks use a variety of cabling options. Non-Ethernet networks, such as Token Ring, rarely use combo cards.

Step 4

a)   10-Base-2 NICs have a BNC connector that attaches to the cable via a T connector.

b)   10-Base-T NICs use RJ-45 connectors.

c)   10-Base-FX NICs use either SC or ST connectors.

d)   Token Ring NICs use either the older female 9-pin DB connectors or the newer RJ-45 connectors.

Lab 8.02 Solution

Step 6 To view the location of the newly installed NIC, open the Control Panel, as indicated in Figure 8-6.

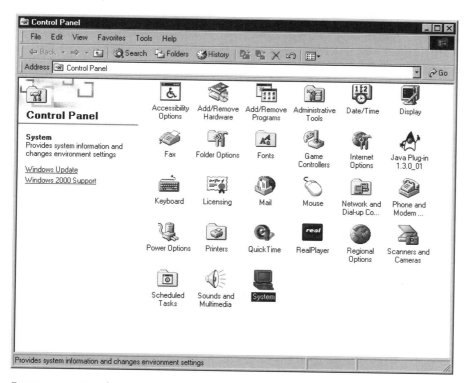

FIGURE 8-6 Windows 2000 Control Panel

The Device Manager is found on the Hardware tab of the computer's System Properties as indicated in Figure 8-7.

Expanding the Network Adapters object in the Device Manager will show the NICs installed on your computer as indicated in Figure 8-8.

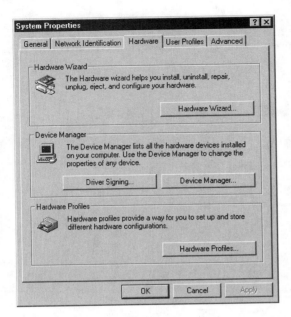

FIGURE 8-7 System Properties

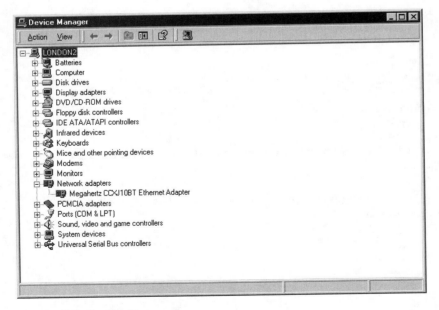

FIGURE 8-8 Device Manager

Step 7 You can double-click on the network adapter that you have installed and view the properties as indicated in Figure 8-9.

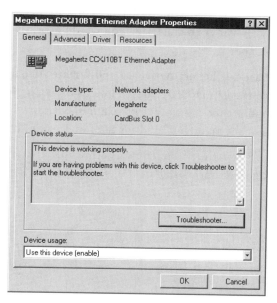

FIGURE 8-9 NIC properties

Answers to Lab Analysis

1. Most NICs will have lights on them that provide different functions. One light is a link (connection) light that tells you if the NIC is connected to a hub. The second light is an activity light that will flicker when network traffic is detected by the NIC. To determine if the NIC is functional, you may try to send or copy a file and then view these lights.

2. It is not always possible to tell the network technology that a NIC with an RJ-45 connector is used for, just by viewing the NIC. If the NIC has some printed information on it, this will help you determine the technology. For example, "Token Link" indicates that it is used for a Token Ring network. Most often, manufacturers of Token Ring NICs will give them a Token Ring–sounding name, which will greatly aid you in your determination. Additionally, you may view the value 16/4 on the card, which indicates a Token Ring NIC. The 16 denotes 16 Mbps and the 4 denotes 4 Mbps.

3. If a NIC is not an available option, you can use a modem to dial into a network. You can also connect two PCs together via a direct cable connection. You can string a null modem cable between the two serial ports (RS-232/DB-9 male connectors) of the PCs enabling them to share the information on their shared hard drives. Both methods of connecting to a network are significantly slower than the speed you would attain through using a NIC, but significantly cheaper in cost.

4. Female DB-15 connectors are used on 10-Base-2 Ethernet networks and female DB-9 are used on older Token Ring cards. These are the common DB connectors that may be found in today's network environments. Remember that the Network+ exam may try and confuse you by showing you DB-25 connectors that are often used for SCSI or parallel ports.

5. Fiber Distributed Data Interface connectors are large, flat, square connectors that are used with the FDDI topology that includes fiber optic cables.

Answers to Key Term Quiz

1. null modem cable

2. Centronics connectors

3. RJ-45 connectors

4. auto-sensing NICs

5. combo card

Chapter 9

Structured Cabling

Lab Exercises

Most networks today consist of more than one hub and/or switch and a few network cables connecting the computers, servers, and printers on the network. In reality, most networks combine different cabling, multiple hardware devices, and even multiple (hybrid) topologies. Networks can get messy, from a connectivity point of view, with all of these different devices, and the goal of most network designers is to implement a solution that will adhere to the standards of the Electronic Industries Association and the Telecommunications Industry Association (EIA/TIA), as well as organize the cabling and devices so that designers can identify where the problems lay. The EIA/TIA define several aspects of installing cabling in buildings and have developed a standard for structured cabling. In this chapter, we will examine the EIA/TIA recommendations and look at how we can implement their recommendations in various network settings.

 60 MINUTES

Lab 9.01: Examining Horizontal Cabling

Your company is moving into a new building and they will be completely rebuilding the network infrastructure, which includes creating a new equipment room, installing client computers and servers, and installing cabling. The intent is to implement an Ethernet network with a physical star topology as an inexpensive solution. Your network is currently using 4-wire Category 5 UTP Plenum cabling. This cabling is suspended above dropped ceilings and no work area is more than 90 meters away from the equipment room. The equipment room in the new building will also maintain the same distance from the work area to the equipment room. You are not sure why they are using this type of cabling and wonder if there are other options available that they should consider before installation begins. You decide to research the current cabling solution and explore additional horizontal cabling options.

Learning Objectives

In this lab, you'll learn about horizontal cabling. At the end of this lab, you will be able to

- Define the EIA/TIA standards for horizontal cabling
- Identify the implementation of each type of horizontal cabling

Lab Materials and Setup

For this lab exercise, you'll need

- Pencil and paper
- Internet access

Getting Down to Business

Step 1 List the three different types of cable approved by the EIA/TIA for horizontal cabling. What common type of cable is not approved for horizontal cabling?

_____

_____

_____

Step 2 Research on the Internet to determine the features of your company's UTP Plenum Category 5 horizontal cabling and list them in the space provided here.

_____

_____

Step 3   How does the implementation of this UTP cabling differ from the other horizontal cabling options? Define the features of the other horizontal cabling options and describe how to implement these cables.

_____

_____

Step 4   Based on your findings, what is the best cabling option for your company? Why?

_____

_____

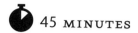 45 MINUTES

Lab 9.02: Comparing Cabling Equipment

DGK Technologies would like to expand their basic 10-Base-T network to include several new client computers and servers, yet they have run out of available ports on their current hub. They are considering implementing cascading hubs yet they know that the additional computers will slow down network traffic when they are simply using hubs to provide connectivity. They have also looked at the option of using several switches instead of hubs to provide for expansion. They realize that this option can be very expensive and therefore, they are still unsure of what is the best solution for expanding their basic star network.

Learning Objectives

In this lab, you'll examine and compare the cabling equipment used in today's networks. At the end of this lab, you will be able to

- Understand the new basic star topology

- Compare hubs and switches

- Identify backbone cabling

Lab Materials and Setup

For this lab exercise, you'll need

- Pencil and paper

- Internet access

Getting Down to Business

Step 1   Research on the Internet to discover the advantages and disadvantages of expanding a basic star network with the use of cascading hubs. List your findings here.

Step 2   Research on the Internet to discover the advantages and disadvantages of using switches to expand a basic star network. List your findings here.

_____

_____

Step 3   What other options are available to DGK Technologies that would provide expansion and combat a slow network?

_____

_____

Step 4   What is backbone cabling and what advice does the EIA/TIA recommend when implementing backbone cabling?

_____

_____

Lab Analysis

1.   What type of hardware is typically included in a standard equipment room?

_____

_____

2.   Why does the EIA/TIA standard set the maximum distance from the equipment room to any one work area at 90 meters if most UTP technologies allow for 100 meters?

_____

_____

3.   What three essential components make up a successful implementation of a basic star network when using structured cabling?

_____

_____

4.   What are the six subsystems of a structured cabling system defined by the EIA/TIA?

_____

_____

5.   What type of backbone cabling should be used for inter-building communication?

_____

_____

Key Term Quiz

Use the following vocabulary terms to complete the sentences below. Not all of the terms will be used.

backbone

gauge

impedance

multi-speed hub

patch cables

patch panel

Plenum cable

polyvinyl chloride (PVC) cable

standby power supply (SPS)

switch

uninterruptible power supply (UPS)

1. A _____ is a box with a row of ports to which you connect horizontal cables within the equipment room in order to organize cables and prevent breakage from moving the cables.

2. A _____ does not provide continuous power, it only activates when it detects a power outage.

3. _____ is the amount of resistance to an electrical signal on a wire used to measure the amount of data a cable can handle.

4. _____ possesses a fire-retardant coating so it does not give off toxic gasses and smoke as it burns.

5. A fast and simple solution for too much traffic on a 10-Base-T network is to replace a hub with a _____.

Lab Wrap-Up

Though the Network+ exam will not test you on all aspects of structured cabling and the EIA/TIA standards, it is helpful to know how to design a network from the cabling hardware aspect. Understanding structured cabling makes designing a network solution simpler and helps you understand the hardware that you must include and the limitations of your design solution. You may not become an expert electrician or installer; however, you will definitely be able to break down the installation aspects into components when troubleshooting network problems.

Solutions

In this section, you'll find solutions to the lab exercises, the Lab Analysis questions, and the Key Term Quiz.

Lab 9.01 Solution

Step 1   EIA/TIA 568 recognizes the three following types of horizontal cables:

Four-pair, 100 Ohm, 24 AWG, solid-core UTP

Two-pair, 150 Ohm, 22 AWG, solid-core STP

Two-fiber, 62.5/125μm fiber optic

Coaxial cable is not recommended by the EIA/TIA. You should not use it in structured cabling.

Step 2   The EIA/TIA 568 standard for UTP cabling highly recommends 4-wire Category 5 UTP cabling, as it requires 4 pairs of wires. Category 5 Plenum UTP cabling supports speeds up to 100 Mbps, and has a fire-retardant coating to prevent excess smoke and fumes. It is typically installed above drop ceilings away from fluorescent lights and power cables that cause interference. This cabling, Category 5 Plenum as well as the advanced Category 5(e) cabling is typically installed in many networks.

Step 3   STP, like UTP, is typically installed above drop ceilings on hooks or racks. STP cabling is typically used in Token Ring networks. It is relatively inexpensive, like UTP; however, when implemented, you must ground its shielding. Fiber optic cables are expensive but have the advantage of not using electricity, so there is no interference. It is also more difficult to install than the other two cabling options, as it is quite fragile. A good understanding of the six subsystems of a structured cabling system can be found at www.anixter.com/techlib/standard/cabling/d0502p09.htm#2.

Step 4   Based on the available cabling options, the best solution for the company would be the Category 5 Plenum UTP cabling that is currently being implemented. This cabling is relatively inexpensive, easy to install, and provides a high rate of data transfer.

Lab 9.02 Solution

Step 1   Cascading hubs offer the advantages of linking hubs together to expand a network. You can connect two or more hubs via crossover cables or with a regular cable when using the crossover ports available on most of today's hubs. The disadvantage of simply adding several hubs to expand your network is that the more computers that you have attached to the hubs, the more the network performance may slow down due to the increased network traffic.

Step 2 Switches, though they look similar to hubs, provide a hardware solution to improve network performance with bridging capabilities. Switches filter traffic through MAC addresses and segment networks into different subnets. Segmenting the network into one or more subnets keeps one network from overloading with traffic. Switches are still more expensive than hubs, but their prices have decreased in the last few years. Switches can eliminate most collision problems on a network through replacing hubs; however, the performance may not be significant enough to justify the cost of changing all hubs on your networks to switches.

Step 3 Implementing a central switch on a multi-hub network may be a viable option to increasing the size of a network without having any degradation in performance. This is an inexpensive option that provides the ability to connect servers directly to the switch, so the traffic intended for them is sent to them directly. The switch also provides for the filtering of packets from hub to hub.

Another option to implement may be a high-speed network, replacing all the 10-Base-T NICs with 100-Base-T devices, but this is not a cost-effective solution. Multi-speed 10/100 Mbps hubs will solve this problem by allowing servers to communicate at 100 Mbps and the client computers communicate at 10 Mbps.

Step 4 The backbone cabling provides the communication between the hubs, switches, servers, equipments rooms, and cabling closets. UTP and fiber optic cables are most often chosen for backbones, and they are used to vertically connect equipment rooms in buildings (UTP) and horizontally connect buildings (fiber optic). The EIA/TIA specifies how building entrances must be configured. You will not need to know this for the Network+ exam, but you can refer to the specifications at www.anixter.com/techlib/standard/cabling/do502po8.htm#3.

Answers to Lab Analysis

1. The equipment room contains the telephone equipment and all the cables that connect to the hubs, switches, or routers that are usually mounted on equipment racks. It may also contain an uninterruptible power supply or standby power supply and several patch panels.

2. Though the EIA/TIA standard sets the maximum distance from the equipment room to any one work area at 90 meters and most UTP technologies allow for 100 meters, there is no discrepancy in this area. The extra 10 meters allow for the extra distance between the hub and the PC used by the patch cables.

3. An equipment room, horizontal cabling, and a work area make up the basic star network. The cabling must run to the equipment room, where it connects to an MSAU, a hub, or a telephone system. The cables then run horizontally from the equipment room

to the computers in the work area. The work area can be a simple wall outlet that has female jacks to accept the incoming cabling from the computers.

4. The six subsystems of a structured cabling system as defined by the EIA/TIA are the building entrance, equipment room, backbone cabling, telecommunications closet, horizontal cabling, and work area.

5. Fiber optic cabling is the only backbone cabling that you should use between buildings, as it is not affected by electrical interference.

Answers to Key Term Quiz

1. patch panel

2. standby power supply (SPS)

3. impedance

4. Plenum cable

5. switch

Chapter 10
Dealing with the Physical

Lab Exercises

Dealing with the physical aspects of a network includes installing a structured cabling system. This may include planning the installation, pulling and connecting the cables, and testing the connections to ensure that your installation is successful. These may not be the typical tasks of a network administrator; however, your greater knowledge about the physical structure of your network will help when you are troubleshooting connection problems.

In this chapter, we will look at all aspects of installing a structured cabling system, from the planning of the system to the pulling and connecting of cables. We will also identify a variety of tools that are used to test cable runs and trace cables.

 30 MINUTES

Lab 10.01: Planning an Installation of a Physical Network

BJC Industries has hired you to design a basic structured cabling system for their new office location in Denver. They wish to have a complete physical installation of all client computers, servers, cabling, and other hardware. Their requirements state that this is to be a single-floor office in a newly built office building. This is your first physical design project, and you want to make sure that you are considering all the steps involved before presenting your design to the company.

Learning Objectives

In this lab, you'll plan an installation of a physical network. At the end of this lab, you will be able to

- Recognize the steps involved in planning an installation

- Identify the factors involved in determining an equipment room location

- Identify common equipment room contents

Lab Materials and Setup

For this lab exercise, you'll need

- Pencil and paper

- Internet access

- Accessible equipment room (optional)

Getting Down to Business

Step 1   What steps should you consider when planning a physical installation of structured cabling for BJC Industries?

✔ **Hint**

Consider the structure of the building and how it affects your physical design.

_____

_____

Step 2   What factors should you consider when determining where BJC Industries' equipment room should be located?

_____

_____

Step 3   Research on the Internet, or visit an equipment room if you have access to one, to determine common hardware found in a typical equipment room. List your findings here.

_____

_____

 60 MINUTES

Lab 10.02: Pulling Cabling

BJC Industries has approved your design for the physical installation of their network. They wish for the installation to begin immediately. The first task is pulling the cable that their network will use. You determine that this task is beyond your capabilities, and you decide to hire professionals to complete the job. You plan to observe the work of the cable installers to learn the components and methods they use.

Learning Objectives

In this lab, you'll examine the process of pulling cabling on a single floor in a single building. At the end of this lab, you will be able to

- Identify the components used to pull cable

- Describe the methods used by professional cable installers

Lab Materials and Setup

For this lab exercise, you'll need

- Pencil and paper

- Internet access

Getting Down To Business

Step 1   What tools do professionals have at their disposal to help them pull cables? Research on the Internet to find examples of these tools and list your findings and references here.

_____

_____

Step 2   The EIA/TIA has strict rules regarding how cables are pulled. Research on the Internet to discover these rules and list three of the rules here.

_____

_____

Step 3 What are the steps a professional installer would likely take when dropping and connecting cables? Research on the Internet for any additional information you may need.

✔ **Hint**

Consider the entire process from the beginning location to the destination connection at the work area.

Lab Analysis

1. What factors should you consider in terms of cable management after you have installed your structured cabling system?

    _____

    _____

2. Why is labeling the cabling so important in a network installation?

    _____

    _____

3. What tool is often used to connect the cable to the jack after the cable has been dropped to the work area?

    _____

    _____

4. What factor may determine a decision to run cabling externally rather than inside the walls? How do you accomplish this?

    _____

    _____

5. What are Cat 5 cable testing tools and how would they aid you when installing and testing a structured cabling system?

    _____

    _____

Key Term Quiz

Use the following vocabulary terms to complete the sentences below. Not all of the terms will be used.

cable drop

CAT 5 cable tester

continuity testers

D-rings

finger boxes

Time Domain Reflectometer (TDR)

tone generator

tone probe

1. A _____ emits a sound when it is placed near a cable connected to the tone generator.

2. A _____ is a location where the cable comes out of the wall.

3. Plastic _____ are sometimes used to guide patch cables neatly along the sides and front of a patch panel.

4. A cable tester that can determine the length of a cable as well as where a break is located is called a _____.

5. A _____ connects to a cable and sends an electrical signal along the wire at a certain frequency.

Lab Wrap-Up

As you have learned, professional installers are often contacted to run and drop cables for networks, as it can be a difficult and unpleasant job. Though you may never experience the actual task of running cables, you should understand the rules that guide the running of cables and the location of the equipment room and work area. You may also encounter difficulties with connections, patch panels, and bad cabling in your network. The ability to recognize what tools will help you discover and resolve these problems will aid you greatly in troubleshooting your network.

Solutions

In this section, you'll find solutions to the lab exercises, the Lab Analysis questions, and the Key Term Quiz.

Lab 10.01 Solution

Step 1   The first thing you need to consider when planning the physical installation for BJC Industries is the floor plan of the new office in Denver. If possible, as this is a new building, obtain the blueprint of the area where you will be physically installing the network cabling and hardware. You need to consider if there are any obstructions to pulling the cabling throughout the proposed area of the office building, such as firewalls.

Second, you need to determine whether you will install the cabling within the walls or outside the walls. As this is a new building, you may consider installing within the walls, especially if there is no evidence of any obstructions.

Third, you need to determine where the equipment room will be located, as well as the work areas.

Step 2   The decision for placement of the equipment room should be based on the EIA/TIA standards that limit the cable length to 90 meters. You should consider placing the equipment room in an accessible location for those who need access, and on its own dedicated power circuit, if at all possible. The room should also have access to air conditioning, especially if you plan on filling it with several servers, and should be large enough to accommodate possible future expansion.

Step 3   These results will vary based on the equipment rooms you visit. Common hardware found in an equipment room may include servers, UPS, hubs, switches, patch panels, patch cables, and wall-mounted racks.

Lab 10.02 Solution

Step 1   Professional cable installers have a variety of tools at their disposal to help them complete their task. To help them pull cable horizontally they may use telescoping poles, special nylon pull strings, fish tapes, crossbows, and pistols. To assist them in dropping cable, they may use a weight attached to the end of a nylon pull rope and cable that would assist them in pulling the cable downwards.

Step 2   Depending on your research, the answers may vary, but the pertinent EIA/TIA standard rules regarding pulling cabling include

- Breaking strength
- Bending radius
- Maximum pulling tension

Step 3   A professional installer might first start the installation at the equipment room, where all cables will typically connect to the back of a patch panel. They may then pull the cabling, using any number of available tools, through the ceiling area, carefully avoiding any previously installed cabling. They may then drop the cable behind the walls to the destination outlet in the work area where they will proceed to install a low-voltage mounting bracket and faceplate. The last step will be crimping an RJ-45 jack onto the end of the wire and mounting the faceplate in the wall.

Answers to Lab Analysis

1.   In terms of cable management, you should consider patch cable management, as it relates to the patch panels in the equipment room. You can use such tools as plastic D-rings and finger boxes to help organize your cabling. Consider different colored cabling to help distinguish cables from one another. You should also organize the layout of your patch panels so they mirror your network either physically or logically—by user groups, companies, or departments.

2.   It is extremely important to label your cabling and connections, both at the patch panel and at the wall outlet, to prevent any connection confusion and to ensure that both ends of the cable are labeled correctly.

3.   Most jacks use the popular 110-punchdown connection. It has a color code that tells you which wire to punch into which connection on the back of the jack. You can use the special 110-punchdown tool to make these connections. You can view a 110-punchdown tool at www.kx-td.com/essentials/tools.asp.

4.   Raceways are products that adhere to your walls, allowing for a simple installation of cables externally. You may choose to use raceways if you don't have the ability or permission to go through the walls to run cables.

5.   Cat 5 cable testers are designed to simplify the tracking and testing of Level 5 network installations. These tools will test UTP cabling and can test Cat 1 through 5 type cables

with RJ-45 connections as well as test fiber optic and coaxial cables. A cable tester can tell you whether installed wiring can support different kinds of networking architecture, such as coaxial, 10-Base-T, 100-Base-T, and Token Ring.

Answers to Key Term Quiz

1. tone probe

2. cable drop

3. D-rings

4. Time Domain Reflectometer (TDR)

5. tone generator

Chapter 11

Protocols

Lab Exercises

For two computers on a network to communicate successfully, they must speak the same language. In the computer industry, these languages are known as network protocols. Even though a computer may have the appropriate network operating system, an operational network interface card (NIC), and the appropriate network cable, communication is not able to occur without the network protocol. You can install more than one network protocol on each computer in the network. In most companies, this is a common occurrence.

In this chapter, we will look at the common NetBEUI protocol and the Internetwork Packet Exchange/Sequenced Packet Exchange (IPX/SPX) compatible protocol.

We will examine adding the NetBEUI protocol to a Windows computer and setting the frame type to the NWLink IPX/SPX/NetBIOS Compatible Transport Protocol. We will discuss the popular TCP/IP protocol suite in the next chapter.

 60 MINUTES

Lab 11.01: Adding the NetBEUI Protocol

GEC Telecommunications has recently hired you as member of the technical support team. Your supervisor calls you on your first day and asks you to ensure that a user's Windows 2000 Professional computer on a small workgroup is able to connect to their Windows 2000 Server. You first check the hardware of the computer and verify that the NIC is installed in the computer and that the network cable plugged into the NIC is operational as indicated by the illuminated link light on the card. You know that the Windows 2000 Server is only running the NetBEUI protocol for the internal network and you wish to ensure that the user's computer is also running this protocol.

Learning Objectives

In this lab, you'll add the network protocol NetBEUI to the network operating system. At the end of this lab, you will be able to

- Identify the location of network protocols

- Bind the NetBEUI protocol to a NIC

Lab Materials and Setup

For this lab exercise, you'll need

- Pencil and paper

- Windows 95, 98, NT, Me, XP, or 2000 computer with a NIC installed

Getting Down to Business

Step 1 Based on the information presented in the case study, can you determine if the Windows 2000 Professional computer is running the NetBEUI protocol without looking at the configuration of the NIC? Why? Could you determine this without viewing the configuration of the NIC if the computer were running a Windows 95 operating system? Why?

✔ **Tech Note**

If you're running a Windows 2000 operating system, continue with Steps 2 through 5. If running any other operating system, proceed to Step 6.

Step 2 From the Windows 2000 desktop, right-click the My Network Places icon and select Properties from the menu.

Step 3 From the available connections in the Network Connections And Dial-Up window, right-click the Local Area Connection icon and select Properties from the menu. The Local Area Connection dialog box should appear, as shown in Figure 11-1.

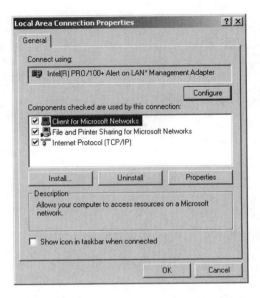

FIGURE 11-1 Local Area Connection

Step 4 In the Local Area Connection dialog box, view and note the name of your NIC and view and note the components installed and used by the NIC connection. Verify that NetBEUI is not installed.

Step 5 Click the Install button and select Protocol in the Select Network Component Type window. Proceed to install the NetBEUI protocol from the list of protocols as shown in Figure 11-2.

Step 6 Where can you view the location of the protocols on your network operating system? From your particular operating system, browse to the installation location of the protocols and note the location and the steps you took to get to that location in the space provided here.

_____

_____

FIGURE 11-2 Select Network Component Type

Step 7   In the case of GEC Telecommunications, why is it important that both the Windows 2000 Server and Windows 2000 Professional computer be running the NetBEUI protocol?

_____

_____

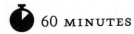 60 MINUTES

Lab 11.02: Setting the IPX/SPX Frame Type

You are troubleshooting a connection problem between a Windows 98 computer and a Novell Netware server. You know that the Novell Netware server is running the IPX/SPX protocol and that the Windows 98 computer is running the NWLink IPX/SPX/NetBIOS Compatible Transport Protocol. You suspect the problem may be that the IPX/SPX protocol is configured to one frame type for the client computer and a different frame type for the server.

Learning Objectives

In this lab, you'll examine the IPX/SPX protocol frame type. At the end of this lab you will be able to

- Install the NWLink IPX/SPX/NetBIOS Compatible Transport Protocol
- Manually set the IPX/SPX frame type

Lab Materials and Setup

For this lab exercise, you'll need

- Pencil and paper
- Internet access

Getting Down to Business

 Tech Note

This lab requires that you complete some steps on your own, without step-by-step instructions.

Step 1 Use the knowledge that you acquired in the previous lab to install the NWLink IPX/SPX/NetBIOS Compatible Transport Protocol and ensure that it is installed for your network card.

✔ **Tech Note**

If you have a modem installed, ensure that the protocol is bound to the NIC, and not the modem.

Step 2   Once the protocol has been installed, choose to view the Properties of the protocol and then choose to manually select the frame type. Select the 802.3 frame type.

Step 3   What other frame types are available to be chosen? List the frame types here.

_____

_____

Step 4   Research on the Internet and determine the function of the IPX/SPX frame type and how it affects communication on the network. List your findings in the space provided here.

_____

_____

Lab Analysis

1. What are the primary characteristics of the NetBEUI protocol?

_____

_____

2. What are the primary characteristics of the IPX/SPX protocol?

_____

_____

3. What purpose would require some computer systems on a network to run a different protocol from others?

_____

_____

4. If you had more than one NIC installed on a computer, is it possible to bind a different protocol to each NIC? If so, why would this feature be useful?

_____

_____

5. Does Microsoft's implementation of the IPX/SPX protocol allow you to connect to Microsoft computers, or simply Novell NetWare computers?

_____

_____

Key Term Quiz

Use the following vocabulary terms to complete the sentences below. Not all of the terms will be used.

AppleTalk

binding

Data Link Control (DLC)

domain name service (DNS)

frame type

Internetwork Packet Exchange/Sequenced Packet Exchange (IPX/SPX)

NetBEUI

NetBIOS

NetWare Core Protocol (NCP)

NWLink

Request for Comments (RFC)

Service Advertising Protocol (SAP)

Transmission Control Protocol/Internet Protocol (TCP/IP)

1. _____ is a fast, simple, non-routable set of network protocols used by Microsoft network operating systems.

2. If computers using the _____ protocol suite use different frame types, they will not be able to communicate.

3. A document known as a _____ defines each protocol within the TCP/IP suite of protocols.

4. The process of assigning a protocol to a specific NIC is known as _____.

5. The _____ protocol manages connections between computers based on the names of the computers involved.

Lab Wrap-Up

As you have learned, the process of adding and configuring both the NetBEUI and IPX/SPX protocol is fairly straightforward. If you run into problems and need to troubleshoot connectivity in regards to the protocol binding, it is recommended that you simply reinstall the protocol. The important thing to remember is that the correct protocols for the network environment are installed on the appropriate client computers. The TCP/IP protocol suite requires additional configuration and, therefore, we will spend the next chapter looking at it in detail.

Solutions

In this section, you'll find solutions to the lab exercises, the Lab Analysis questions, and the Key Term Quiz.

Lab 11.01 Solution

Step 1 Without viewing the configuration of the NIC, it is impossible to determine if the Windows 2000 Professional computer has the NetBEUI protocol installed. NetBEUI is not installed by default on a Windows 2000 computer; therefore, you must check the configuration of the NIC. If the computer were running a Windows 95 operating system, you could possibly determine whether or not the NetBEUI protocol was installed, without viewing the NIC configuration. NetBEUI is installed by default in a Windows 95 operating system. If the protocol had not been manually removed, you could assume that it was installed. However, it is best to *always* check the configuration of the connection to ensure that the protocol is installed on the local client computer.

Step 6 Answers will vary depending upon the network operating system used. For Windows 2000 systems, the protocols can be found by executing the following steps:

1. Right-click and select Properties from the My Network Places menu.

2. Right-click and select Properties from the Local Area Connection.

3. Click the Install button in the Select Network Component Type dialog box.

4. Select Protocol.

   For a Windows 95/98 system, the protocols can be found by executing the following steps:

1. Right-click the Network Neighborhood Icon and select Properties.

2. Click the Add button in the Network dialog box.

3. Select Protocol.

Step 7 For the Windows 2000 Professional computer to communicate with the Windows 2000 Server computer successfully, it must have the same network protocol installed as is running on the server—in this case, NetBEUI. If the protocols are not the same, the computers will not be able to communicate.

Lab 11.02 Solution

Step 3 The other frame types available are Ethernet 802.2, Ethernet II, and Ethernet SNAP.

Step 4 The IPX/SPX frame type determines the order and type of data included in each packet being delivered on the network. An informative article can be found at www. networkmagazine.com/article/NMG20000727S0013.

Answers to Lab Analysis

1. The NetBEUI protocol suite is made up of two protocols: NetBIOS and NetBEUI. It is a fast, simple Microsoft protocol that is non-routable and therefore used only in small network settings. NetBIOS and Net BEUI operate at the Session layer and the Transport layer of the OSI model, respectively.

2. The IPX/SPX protocol suite, used primarily by Novell NetWare–based networks, is a routable protocol suite that combines the Internetwork Packet Exchange (IPX) and Sequenced Packet Exchange (SPX) protocols. IPX is responsible for routing data packets between networks and operates at the Network layer of the OSI model. SPX operates at the Transport layer of the OSI model and is responsible for breaking data into small packets and reassembling these data packets.

3. By using different protocols, a network administrator can guarantee that two sets of computer systems on the same network cannot access each other. This may be necessary for security reasons. For example, Computers A and B both run the IPX/SPX protocol and Computers C and D use the NetBEUI protocol. This would mean that Computers A and B can communicate with each other, but they cannot communicate with Computers C and D, and vice versa.

4. It is possible to bind different protocols to different NICs if you have more than one NIC in a computer system. The ability to do this provides extra security, especially if you are using one NIC to access an external network, such as the Internet, and one NIC for the internal network.

5. You can use the NWLink IPX/SPX/NetBIOS Compatible Transport Protocol to connect to both Microsoft network operating systems as well as Novell NetWare operating systems.

Answers to Key Term Quiz

1. NetBEUI

2. IPX/SPX

3. Request for Comments (RFC)

4. binding

5. NetBIOS

Chapter 12

TCP/IP

Lab Exercises

Tcp/IP is a de facto industry-standard suite of protocols, but is most often recognized as the Internet protocol. It is designed for wide area networks (WANs) and as a result is a routable protocol. TCP/IP uses several protocols, aside from the two primary protocols TCP and IP. It is important that you understand the entire suite of protocols and their functions in today's networks.

In this chapter, we will look at a wide variety of TCP/IP-related issues. We will examine binary and decimal IP addresses and subnet masks. We will also configure TCP/IP with a static IP address, subnet mask, and default gateway. Finally, we will identify various key ports that are used for communication.

60 MINUTES

Lab 12.01: Examining Binary and Decimal IP Addresses

Your supervisor has asked you to define the IP addresses for all 200 computers on the company network. He has informed you that he needs a written copy of all addresses in both decimal and binary format for future segmenting of the network. To complete his request, you must be able to recognize valid IP addresses and convert them from binary to decimal and vice versa. You decide to practice recognizing and converting IP addresses.

Learning Objectives

In this lab, you'll examine IP addresses in both binary and decimal number format. At the end of this lab, you will be able to

- Recognize valid IP addresses

- Convert binary values to decimal values

- Convert decimal values to binary values
- Identify IP address classes

Lab Materials and Setup

For this lab exercise, you'll need

- Pencil and paper
- Scientific calculator (optional)
- Internet access

Getting Down to Business

Step 1 Identify whether the following IP addresses are valid or invalid in the following list. Give reasons for the invalid IP addresses.

IP Address	Valid/Invalid
a) 131.107.2.224	_____
b) 255.255.3.98	_____
c) 169.253.78.23	_____
d) 1.3.6.10	_____
e) 254.224.204	_____
f) 127.0.0.1	_____
g) 255.255.255.255	_____
h) 125.34.228.49	_____
i) 0.0.0.0	_____
j) 189.34.127.255	_____

Step 2 Convert the following IP addresses into binary format in the following list.

IP Address   **Binary Format**

a) 134.105.23.5   _____

b) 185.34.67.223   _____

c) 34.68.13.216   _____

d) 235.236.12.24   _____

e) 253.17.88.33   _____

f) 217.189.173.125   _____

g) 221.28.178.145   _____

h) 175.27.192.126   _____

i) 173.122.179.26   _____

j) 145.174.128.46   _____

Step 3 Convert the following binary IP addresses to decimal format.

Binary IP Address   **Decimal Format**

a) 11111010 10111100 01110110 11101011   _____

b) 01101101 11101011 11111101 11001100   _____

c) 00000011 10000011 10101010 00011101   _____

d) 00001111 01001111 10011110 11111110   _____

e) 00111100 01110001 01100011 01111000   _____

f) 00001010 10011110 00111011 11000011   _____

g) 11100011 00011100 00111111 11011010   _____

h) 10001011 10011110 11101111 10111111   _____

i) 11110111 00100000 00011011 11111000   _____

j) 11111100 11111011 10111011 11111011   _____

Step 4 Is 000111 1011 111 11 a valid IP address? Give reasons for your answer.

_____

_____

Step 5 For each IP addresses listed here, indicate the class of the address.

IP Address	Class
a) 134.105.23.5	_____
b) 185.34.67.223	_____
c) 34.68.13.216	_____
d) 235.236.12.24	_____
e) 253.17.88.33	_____
f) 217.189.173.125	_____
g) 221.28.178.145	_____
h) 175.27.192.126	_____
i) 173.122.179.26	_____
j) 145.174.128.46	_____

 45 MINUTES

Lab 12.02: Understanding Subnet Masks

Your company is assigned a Class B network ID of 165.1.0.0. By the end of the year, the network will need to support 16 subnets. Your supervisor has asked you to ensure that you choose a proper subnet mask to provide support for a maximum number of hosts per subnet. To determine the appropriate subnet mask, you review your knowledge of subnet masks and how they function.

Learning Objectives

In this lab, you'll examine the process of assigning a subnet mask to an IP address. At the end of this lab, you will be able to

- Recognize default subnet masks

- Identify network and host IDs

- Define a custom subnet mask

- Determine local and remote hosts

Lab Materials and Setup

For this lab exercise, you'll need

- Pencil and paper

- Scientific calculator

- Internet access

Getting Down to Business

Step 1   Define the default subnet masks for Class A, B, and C.

_____

_____

Step 2   Based on the default subnet masks for the classes in Step 1, identify the network and host IDs for the following IP addresses:

IP Address	Network ID	Host ID
a) 131.194.192.3	_____	_____
b) 45.200.49.201	_____	_____
c) 194.39.110.183	_____	_____

Step 3   Based on your knowledge of subnet masks in Steps 1 and 2, what would the default subnet mask be for your company network? How many hosts does the default subnet mask provide per subnet? Will this satisfy your supervisor's request?

_____

_____

Step 4   Which subnet mask should you use to provide the maximum number of hosts per subnet, for the 16 subnets of your company?

_____

_____

Step 5   Your supervisor has also asked you to determine if the following computers are on the same subnet. Their IP addresses are

Computer A IP Address	10011011 10101010 00100101 10100011
Computer A Subnet Mask	11111111 11111111 00000000 00000000
Computer B IP Address	11011011 10101010 10101000 11101001
Computer B Subnet Mask	11111111 11111111 00000000 00000000

Are the computers on the same or different subnets?

_____

_____

 30 MINUTES

Lab 12.03: Configuring TCP/IP

You wish to give all the devices on your network a static IP address and associated subnet mask so that they can communicate with each other.

Learning Objectives

In this lab, you'll examine the process of assigning a static IP address to a local area connection. At the end of this lab, you will be able to

- Identify the options for obtaining IP addresses
- Assign a static IP address
- Assign a subnet mask to an IP address

Lab Materials and Setup

For this lab exercise, you'll need

- Pencil and paper
- Computer with a Windows operating system
- Internet access

Getting Down to Business

Step 1 Browse to your local area connection and view the TCP/IP protocol properties. Note the steps that you took to reach the location of the TCP/IP properties in the space provided here.

_____

_____

Step 2 What options are available for obtaining an IP address?

_____

_____

Step 3   When assigning an IP address, what basic configuration information can you provide?

_____

_____

Step 4   What is a default gateway and what is its function?

_____

_____

Step 5   Is it necessary to provide a default gateway with every static IP address? Provide the rationale for your answer.

_____

_____

 30 MINUTES

Lab 12.04: Identifying TCP Ports

Your company's users are complaining that they cannot see web pages when viewing through their web browsers. You know that your network contains a web server that delivers pages to the clients. You suspect the problem has to do with the HTTP protocol. You cannot remember which port is used by HTTP and decide to research on the Internet to learn more about what ports are used for transferring data by different protocols.

Learning Objectives

In this lab, you'll examine TCP ports. At the end of this lab, you will be able to

- Define the function of a port

- Identify the ranges of port numbers

- Identify the port numbers of protocols

Lab Materials and Setup

For this lab exercise, you'll need

- Pencil and paper

- Internet access

Getting Down to Business

Step 1 Research on the Internet how ports are used for network communication and how they are classified. Record your results.

_____

_____

Step 2 Identify the following TCP protocol ports.

Protocol	Port
SMTP	_____
TFTP	_____
FTP	_____
HTTP	_____
POP3	_____
NNTP	_____
HTTPS	_____

Step 3 What is the function of HTTP and how would a wrong port number affect communication?

_____

_____

Lab Analysis

1. What are private IP addresses? What IP address ranges are designated as private IP addresses?

_____

_____

2. What is the purpose of defining a DNS server when configuring a static IP address?

_____

_____

3. What is the advantage of configuring a computer to obtain an IP address automatically from a DHCP server?

_____

_____

4. Which protocol is used to transfer data files between servers and clients? Is this supported between different operating systems?

_____

_____

5. Define and explain the process of determining whether a packet is destined for a computer on a local or remote network.

_____

_____

Key Term Quiz

Use the following vocabulary terms to complete the sentences below. Not all of the terms will be used.

Address Resolution Protocol (ARP)

default gateway

Domain Name System (DNS)

Dynamic Host Configuration Protocol (DHCP)

host ID

Post Office Protocol (POP)

Simple Mail Transport Protocol (SMTP)

Simple Network Management Protocol (SNMP)

socket

subnet mask

User Datagram Protocol (UDP)

Windows Internet Naming Service (WINS)

1. A _____ is made up of an IP address and a port number.

2. The service that provides NetBIOS name resolution for a network is known as _____.

3. _____ is a connectionless protocol that is used for broadcasting messages over a network.

4. _____ can be used to assign IP addresses to devices on a network.

5. A _____ is used to determine what segment of a network a host belongs to.

Lab Wrap-Up

Communication between different network environments is essential in the industry today. TCP/IP provides efficient and reliable communication across a variety of platforms and the Internet. You should now have a better understanding of the operation of the protocol suites, the configuration of the TCP/IP protocol, and the process of assigning IP addresses and subnet masks to various network segments on your LAN or WAN. TCP/IP is a de facto industry standard that is still advancing through the introduction of IPv6. Network administrators can look forward to working with this new addressing scheme, as it is expected to gradually replace our current version, IPv4, in the years ahead.

Solutions

In this section, you'll find solutions to the lab exercises, the Lab Analysis questions, and the Key Term Quiz.

Lab 12.01 Solution

Step 1

IP Address	Valid/Invalid
a) 131.107.2.224	Valid
b) 255.255.3.98	Valid
c) 169.253.78.23	Valid
d) 1.3.6.10	Valid
e) 254.224.204	Invalid—only three numbers where there should be four
f) 127.0.0.1	Invalid—reserved for loopback address
g) 255.255.255.255	Invalid—broadcast address as it contains all 255s
h) 125.34.228.49	Valid
i) 0.0.0.0	Invalid—contains all zeros
j) 189.34.127.255	Valid

Step 2

IP Address	Binary Format
a) 134.105.23.5	10000110 01101001 00010111 00000101
b) 185.34.67.223	10111001 00100010 01000011 11011111
c) 34.68.13.216	00100010 00100010 00001101 11011000
d) 235.236.12.24	11101011 11101100 00001100 00011000
e) 253.17.88.33	11111101 00010001 01011000 00100001
f) 217.189.173.125	11011001 10111101 10101101 01111101
g) 221.28.178.145	11011101 00011100 10110010 10010001
h) 175.27.192.126	10101111 00011011 11000000 01111110
i) 173.122.179.26	10101101 01111010 10110011 00011010
j) 145.174.128.46	10010001 10101110 10000000 00101110

Step 3

Binary IP Address	Decimal Format
a) 11111010 10111100 01110110 11101011	250.188.118.235
b) 01101101 11101011 11111101 11001100	109.235.253.204
c) 00000011 10000011 10101010 00011101	3.131.170.29
d) 00001111 01001111 10011110 11111110	15.79.158.254
e) 00111100 01110001 01100011 01111000	60.113.99.120
f) 00001010 10011110 00111011 11000011	10.158.59.195
g) 11100011 00011100 00111111 11011010	227.28.63.218
h) 10001011 10011110 11101111 10111111	139.158.239.191
i) 11110111 00100000 00011011 11111000	247.32.27.248
j) 11111100 11111011 10111011 11111011	252.251.187.251

Step 4   00011 1011 111 11 is a valid address. It converts to a decimal notation of 7.11.7.3, which is a valid IP address. Even though the binary address does not have 8 bits defined, you are to assume that the missing bits are 0s that appear to the left of the numbers shown.

Step 5

IP Address	Class
a) 134.105.23.5	Class B
b) 185.34.67.223	Class C
c) 34.68.13.216	Class A
d) 235.236.12.24	Class D
e) 253.17.88.33	Class E
f) 217.189.173.125	Class C
g) 221.28.178.145	Class C
h) 175.27.192.126	Class B
i) 173.122.179.26	Class B
j) 145.174.128.46	Class B

Lab 12.02 Solution

Step 1

Class A: 255.0.0.0

Class B: 255.255.0.0

Class C: 255.255.255.0

Step 2

IP Address	Network ID	Host ID
a) 131.194.192.3	131.194.0.0	192.3
b) 45.200.49.201	45.0.0.0	200.49.201
c) 194.39.110.183	194.39.110.0	183

Step 3 The default subnet mask for your company's network would be 255.255.0.0, as the company has a Class B network ID. This subnet mask provides 65,534 hosts per subnet. This will not satisfy your supervisor's request, as the default subnet mask only provides for one subnet of 65,534 and cannot be divided into smaller subnets without changing the subnet mask.

Step 4 You would have to use the subnet mask of 255.255.248.0 to provide the maximum hosts for your 16-subnet company network. This custom subnet mask provides for 2,046 hosts per subnet with a network ID of 165.1.0.0. You can determine this subnet mask by converting the number of subnets (16) into binary 00010000 and then converting the number of bits used (5) to determine the mask (11111000) of 248, giving a Class B custom subnet mask of 255.255.248.0.

Step 5

Computer A AND result: 10011011 10101010 00000000 00000000

Computer B AND result: 11011011 10101010 00000000 00000000

Based on the results of ANDing the IP addresses with their subnet masks, the results do not match. Therefore, the two computers are not on the same local subnet.

Lab 12.03 Solution

Step 1 The location of the TCP/IP properties will vary according to the operating system you use. For a Windows 2000 computer, you can access the TCP/IP properties by viewing the properties of My Network Places, then the properties of the local area connection, and finally the properties of the TCP/IP protocol.

Step 2　The options available for obtaining an IP address are to obtain an IP address automatically (through a DHCP server) or by entering a static IP address in the space provided.

Step 3　When assigning a static IP address, you have the option of assigning a subnet mask and default gateway at the same time. Additionally, there is an option to obtain a DNS server address automatically or specify the address of the DNS server to be used for host name resolution.

Step 4　The default gateway provides a default route for TCP/IP computers or devices to use when communicating with other computers or devices on remote networks. In most cases, the default gateway is either a router or computer. It maintains information about the local and remote networks that it services and how hosts on each network can communicate with each other.

Step 5　It is not necessary to provide a default gateway with every static IP address. If you do not need to communicate with a host on a remote network segment, then a default gateway would not be necessary and does not have to be indicated for clients on the local network to communicate.

Lab 12.04 Solution

Step 1　In TCP/IP, the port is used as a point through which applications communicate, identified by the port number. The port numbers are divided into three ranges: Well Known Ports, Registered Ports, and Dynamic and/or Private Ports. The Well Known Ports are those from 0 through 1023. The Registered Ports are those from 1024 through 49151. The Dynamic and/or Private Ports are those from 49152 through 65535.

Step 2

Protocol	Port
SMTP	25
TFTP	69
FTP	21
HTTP	80
POP3	110
NNTP	119
HTTPS	443

Step 3　When a user enters a URL in a browser, this sends an HTTP command to the web server on the network, asking it to return the requested web page. If the HTTP port used for

communication between the client and the server is not the same (the default port being port 80), then communication will not occur and the web page will not be returned to the client.

Answers to Lab Analysis

1. Private IP addresses are addresses that you can use internally on a network, but they are designed so that routers will destroy them, so that they can never be used on the Internet. The IP address ranges that are designated as private IP addresses are

    -   10.0.0.0 through 10.255.255.255

    -   172.16.0.0 through 172.31.0.0

    -   192.168.0.0 through 192.168.255.0

2. You would define the IP address of a DNS server when you want to use that specific server for host name resolution for your client computer. This is useful if there is more than one DNS server available for host resolution and you wish to ensure that only a particular server is used.

3. By configuring a computer to obtain an IP address automatically from a DHCP server, you are eliminating the administrative task of visiting every computer and assigning an IP address and subnet mask. Also, this will allow computers to dynamically update their IP address when their lease expires.

4. The File Transfer Protocol (FTP) is used to transfer data files between servers and clients. It is supported by different operating systems (Windows, Macintosh, UNIX, etc.) and therefore provides an excellent choice for data transfer.

5. The process used to determine whether a packet is destined for a computer on a local or remote network is called ANDing. The computers' IP addresses and subnet masks are ANDed (combining binary 1s and 0s to produce a result set) and compared. If the results are the same, then the packet is destined for a computer on a local network. If the results differ, then the packet is destined for a computer on a remote network.

Answers to Key Term Quiz

1. socket

2. Windows Internet Naming Service (WINS)

3. User Datagram Protocol (UDP)

4. Dynamic Host Configuration Protocol (DHCP)

5. subnet mask

Chapter 13
Network Operating Systems

Lab Exercises

Choosing a network operating system may be a complex task when building your company's first network. Though all operating systems provide the ability to enable users to share resources on the network, not all operating systems meet all the needs of a company. The popular operating systems such as Microsoft Windows, Novell NetWare, and Linux all provide ways of sharing resources in different ways. Microsoft Windows operating systems provide both client and server functionality and the server console while Novell NetWare provides functions only as a server and has no client functionality on the server itself.

In this chapter, you will learn about the popular operating systems and discover the features and functions that they provide. You will compare two popular Microsoft Windows operating systems, analyze different versions of Novell NetWare, and examine the Linux operating system.

 60 MINUTES

Lab 13.01: Comparing Microsoft Windows Network Operating Systems

Burns Electronics currently implements a workgroup environment with 25 Windows 98 computers. Clients are complaining that they cannot always access the resources they need throughout the network due to lack of permissions on the various computers where the network resources are located. They are considering implementing a Windows 2000 domain by keeping the Windows 98 client computers and adding a Windows 2000 Server to the network. They need to know if making these changes will result in a more effective network scenario for their users.

Learning Objectives

In this lab, you'll compare the features of the Windows 98 and 2000 network operating systems. At the end of this lab, you will be able to

- Recognize the features of each network operating system (NOS)

- Compare the method of security used by each system

- Identify the roles of each network operating system (NOS) on a network

Lab Materials and Setup

For this lab exercise, you'll need

- Pencil and paper

- Computer with a Windows 98 network operating system installed

- Computer with a Windows 2000 Server or Advanced Server operating system installed

Getting Down to Business

Step 1 Based on the current Windows 98 workgroup scenario, describe the process that occurs when users try to access a network resource. Use the Windows 98 network operating system to examine the options for the sharing of resources.

_____

_____

Step 2 What key advantages does adding a Windows 2000 domain provide in terms of user access to resources?

_____

_____

Step 3   What protocols or services must exist on the Windows 98 client computers for them to connect to the Windows 2000 Server? View the default configuration of the Windows 98 computer to determine what default protocols and services are installed.

_____

_____

Step 4   Using Windows 2000 Help, find and list five new features provided by the Windows 2000 network operating system. View the default configuration of the Windows 2000 Server computer to determine what default protocols and services are installed.

_____

_____

 60 MINUTES

Lab 13.02: Analyzing Novell NetWare Versions

Your company is considering upgrading their NetWare 3.*x* environment to a newer version of Novell NetWare. Your network is growing and needs support for remote users accessing the network through the Internet. Your supervisor has asked you to present a summary of how implementing a newer version of NetWare will affect the current network structure in terms of security, client access to resources, and server roles. You must provide a brief description of the NetWare operating system versions and the features they offer your company.

Learning Objectives

In this lab, you'll analyze the different versions of Novell NetWare. At the end of this lab, you will be able to

- Recognize the protocols supported by each version of NetWare

- Describe the method of security used by each version of NetWare

- Define the role of a Novell NetWare network operating system on a network

- Recommend a network operating system solution for a small company

Lab Materials and Setup

For this lab exercise, you'll need

- Pencil and paper

- Internet access

Getting Down to Business

Step 1   Based on your knowledge of the NetWare 3.*x* operating system, give a brief description of the role it plays in a network environment and how it manages security.

Step 2 What network protocol(s) does NetWare 3.x support? How is user access to the network affected by the use of the protocol(s)?

_____

_____

Step 3 What recent versions of NetWare are available for network use? Briefly describe the versions and their features. If necessary, use the Internet to help with your research.

_____

_____

Step 4 How would implementing a recent version of NetWare provide simplified user access on your company's network? If necessary, use the Internet to help with your research.

_____

_____

Step 5 Based on your research, what Novell NetWare operating system would you recommend to your supervisor?

_____

_____

 45 MINUTES

Lab 13.03: Examining the Linux Operating System

Your best friend has recently implemented a Linux operating system on his personal home computer. He informs you that it has many great features and recommends that you install this system. You only use your personal computer to access the Internet and run basic software programs. You know very little about the Linux operating system and decide to research on the Internet to determine if it will suit your needs.

Learning Objectives

In this lab, you'll examine the Linux network operating system. At the end of this lab, you will be able to

- Understand the evolution of the Linux operating system
- Describe the features that Linux provides

Lab Materials and Setup

For this lab exercise, you'll need

- Pencil and paper
- Internet access

Getting Down to Business

Step 1 Research on the Internet the history of the Linux operating system and when and where it was developed. Record your results for future reference.

_____

_____

Step 2 What key features does the Linux operating system provide? List three web sites that provide resources for Linux computers.

_____

_____

Step 3 Would the Linux operating system suit your needs as described in the Lab 13.03 scenario?

_____

_____

Lab Analysis

1. When implementing security by using passwords, what considerations must be taken into account to prevent unauthorized access to your network?

   _____

   _____

2. To share resources on Windows 98 systems, what service must be installed? What does installing this service do to the role of the Windows 98 computer?

   _____

   _____

3. Explain the difference between Novell Directory Services (NDS) and Novell's Bindery database?

   _____

   _____

4. What does the term *open source* imply? What network operating system is known as an open source system?

   _____

   _____

5. What configuration would be necessary to connect a Windows 98 client to a NetWare 5.x server?

   _____

   _____

Key Term Quiz

Use the following vocabulary terms to complete the sentences below. Not all of the terms will be used.

access token

Active Directory (AD)

Bindery database

Client for Microsoft Networks

Novell Directory Services (NDS)

Security Access Manager (SAM) database

share-level security

user-level security

user profile

1. Each NetWare 3.x server maintains its own security database known as the _____.

2. Windows 2000 implements a unique directory service known as _____.

3. When connecting to a Microsoft server, a Windows 98 client must have the _____ installed.

4. Windows 98 operating systems implement _____ when acting as servers.

5. An _____ is shown to a server by a user account to gain access to a resource.

Lab Wrap-Up

You should now understand the basic differences between the popular operating systems of Microsoft Windows, Novell NetWare, and Linux. Choosing an operating system for your company or home is never an easy task. Consider all the advantages and disadvantages of each network operating system before making your decision and understand that the best decision may include several different operating systems in one network.

Solutions

In this section, you'll find solutions to the lab exercises, the Lab Analysis questions, and the Key Term Quiz.

Lab 13.01 Solution

Step 1 When users try to access a network resource in a Windows 98 workgroup, users must provide a valid user account and password that exists with the shared resource at the Windows 98 computer location. Based on the network rights assigned to the user, the appropriate access is given. For example, if the user has been granted Read access to a file, he/she will be able to only read the file, and not edit or delete the file. Figure 13-1 shows an example of a folder shared as WheeboPersonnelRecords allowing Full access.

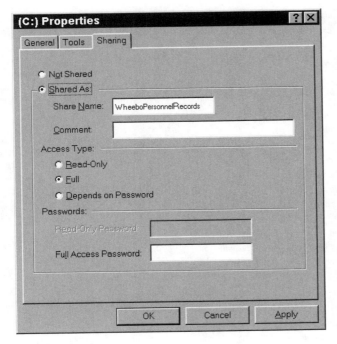

FIGURE 13-1 Windows 98 security options

Windows 98 provides both share-level and user-level security. Share-level security protects shared network resources on the computer running Windows 98 with individually assigned passwords. For example, you can assign a password to a folder or a local printer. If users want to access either resource, they need to type in the appropriate password. If you do not assign a password to a shared resource, every user with access to the network can access that resource. User-level security protects shared network resources by requiring that a user be authenticated to access resources. The security provider, such as a Windows 2000 domain controller, grants access to the shared resource by verifying that the user name and password are the same as those on the user account list stored in Active Directory.

Step 2 By adding a Windows 2000 Server to the company network and implementing a Windows 2000 domain, you can provide centralized user logon and access to network resources. A user can now use a single secure logon account and password, which exists in Active Directory, to access resources anywhere in the network, whether they exist on several different servers. The Active Directory Users and Computers administrative tool, shown in Figure 13-2, provides you with a list of user accounts that exist within the domain.

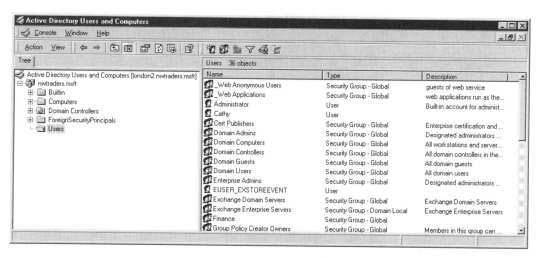

Figure 13-2 Active Directory Users and Computers

Step 3 For the Windows clients to connect to the Windows 2000 Server, the client must be running the same network protocol as the Windows 2000 Server, in many cases TCP/IP. For the users to be authenticated through Active Directory, they must have the add-on Active Directory client software installed. In addition, Windows 98 must have the Client for Microsoft Networks service installed. Figure 13-3 shows the Windows 98 Network dialog box with the Client for Microsoft Networks installed.

Step 4 Windows 2000 Server and Advanced Server provide several key new features, such as Active Directory, Disk Quota Support, Terminal Services, Encrypting File System, and Group Policies. Additional features can be found through the Windows 2000 Help feature.

The default protocols and services installed with Windows 2000 Server and Advanced Server are the Client for Microsoft Networks, File and Printer Sharing for Microsoft Networks, and TCP/IP. Figure 13-4 displays the default Windows 2000 installation of protocols and services.

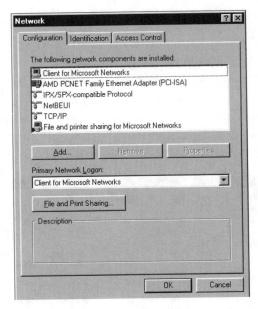

FIGURE 13-3 Windows 98 services and protocols

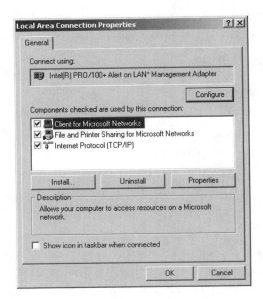

FIGURE 13-4 Windows 2000 services

Lab 13.02 Solution

Step 1 Novell NetWare 3.x is a server operating system. All Novell NetWare servers are true dedicated servers to which clients connect to access shared resources. Clients can receive complete access to the resources on the NetWare 3.x server if their user account and password exist within the server's Bindery database. Each server has its own Bindery database; therefore, if a user needs access to resources on a particular server, he/she must have a valid user account and password in that server's Bindery database to be authenticated. This type of database scheme is known as a server-centric system.

Step 2 Novell NetWare 3.x offers file and print sharing capabilities through the use of the IPX/SPX network protocol suite. Clients using the IPX/SPX protocol can easily connect to the NetWare 3.x server, as this is the primary network protocol supported by NetWare 3.x. The TCP/IP protocol can be added to a NetWare 3.x server for client access, but this is rarely seen in today's network environments so remote client connections through the Internet are rarely seen.

Step 3 Novell NetWare 4.x, 5.x, and 6 are currently available for today's networks.

NetWare 4.x introduced Novell Directory Services (NDS), a directory service that organizes all resource and user information into a centralized security database. This new feature eliminates the need for multiple user accounts and passwords on separate NetWare Servers, as users can now access all resources anywhere on the network from logging onto the directory. This is known as a network-centric system. NetWare 4.x also introduced the support for TCP/IP, allowing IPX/SPX packets to be encapsulated inside TCP/IP packets. Additional information can be viewed at www.cl.cam.ac.uk/Research/Security/resources/BPM/english/b/66.htm.

NetWare 5.x also uses the NDS directory service and is a true TCP/IP platform, which completely removes the need for encapsulation of the IPX/SPX packets inside the TCP/IP packets. TCP/IP clients can connect directly to NetWare 5.x servers and if authenticated, access resources. Additional information can be viewed at www.internetwk.com/news/news081098-4.htm.

The NetWare 6 operating system has recently been released. You can view the features and advantages of this system at www.novell.com/products/netware/.

Step 4 Implementing a recent version of NetWare, such as 5.x or 6, would simplify user access to the network due to the support for the TCP/IP protocol and the NDS directory service. Users will be able to access the servers remotely through the Internet and have access to all network resources through the use of a single secure user account and password.

Step 5 Any of the recent NetWare versions (5.*x* or 6) would provide an optimal solution for the company's needs. The support for TCP/IP would provide for remote user access through the Internet and the NDS directory service would provide for simplified administration and simplified user access to resources.

Lab 13.03 Solution

Step 1 A student, Linus Torvalds, at the University of Helsinki in Finland, initially released the Linux operating system in 1991. The history of the Linux operating system can be found at www.linux.org/info/index.html.

Step 2 The key feature of the Linux operating system is that its source code is available to the public, which allows developers the ability to modify the operating system to meet their needs. The Linux operating system is a stable, reliable, and extremely powerful system. It allows you to share networking CPUs and modems and supports multiple processors. It supports true multitasking and there is a wide variety of software available free of charge.

User access to the Internet is supported through Linux, and there are also a variety of commercially licensed software products available for the Linux operating system.

Linux-related web sites include

- www.linux.com

- www.linuxnewbie.org

- www.portalux.com

- new.linuxnow.com

Step 3 Based on your requirement to access the Internet and run basic software programs, the Linux operating system would suit your needs. Keep in mind, before choosing any operating system, you must research the current computer hardware that you possess and the ease of use, setup, and configuration that the operating system would offer.

Answers to Lab Analysis

1. Password lengths should be at least 6–8 characters and should include both letters and numbers. Users must change their password frequently and rules must be in place to prevent them from using the same passwords over and over again.

2. The File and Print Sharing for Microsoft Networks service must be installed for Windows 98 computers to share network resources. Once you install this on a Windows 98 computer, the role of the computer changes from that of a client to that of a server or client/server.

3. Novell NetWare 3.x Bindery database is a security database that exists on each server and contains a list of user accounts and passwords for that server. Users that are authenticated in the Bindery are able to access all resources on that particular server. Novell Directory Services (NDS) is a centralized (network-centric) security database that contains a list of user accounts and passwords. Users who are authenticated from NDS are able to access all of their resources anywhere on the network.

4. Linux is an open source operating system that gives anyone who purchases the system free access to the source code so that they may modify the operating system, if required, to meet their company's needs.

5. Microsoft provides the Microsoft Client for NetWare Networks for Windows 98 computers wishing to connect to NetWare servers. This service requires the IPX/SPX-compatible transport protocol; however, it does not support connecting to a server running NDS, which is what Novell NetWare 5.x provides. Therefore, Novell's Client32 can be installed on the Windows 98 computer, as it provides access to NetWare servers using either TCP/IP or IPX/SPX and provides full support for NDS.

Answers to Key Term Quiz

1. Bindery database

2. Active Directory (AD)

3. Client for Microsoft Networks

4. share-level security

5. access token

Chapter 14

Resources

Lab Exercises

Sharing resources is the main goal of a computer network. To share or access resources successfully, you must have the appropriate permissions to do so. In this chapter, we will look at sharing both folders and printers over a network. We will work with the Microsoft Windows environment for these labs, as the Network+ exam stresses the sharing process in a Windows environment. We will also examine the Windows NT File System (NTFS) permissions that enable an administrator to assign additional levels of security to the various network resources.

Windows is not the only operating system available today, and therefore, it is necessary that you familiarize yourself with the process of sharing and accessing resources on other operating systems such as Novell NetWare and UNIX/Linux. The *Network+ All-in-One Certification Exam Guide, Second Edition* will assist you in providing additional information on these common network operating systems.

 45 MINUTES

Lab 14.01: Sharing and Accessing a Folder with Windows 2000

It is your first day as the sole network administrator of CMG Toys. Your supervisor has asked you to ensure that the Products folder is available to the Everyone group so that potential clients can view the products when accessing the files through the Internet. Your supervisor also wants other users on the CMG Toys internal network to be able to access these files through mapped drives, UNC paths, and network places. You attempt to share the folder and access it from a computer on your local network.

Learning Objectives

In this lab, you'll examine the process of sharing and accessing a folder with Windows 2000. At the end of this lab, you will be able to

- Share a folder

- Map a network drive

- Access a shared folder through My Network Places

- Access a shared folder by using a Universal Naming Convention (UNC) path

Lab Materials and Setup

For this lab exercise, you'll need

- Pencil and paper

- Two computers that are on the same network and able to communicate with each other

  - Computer A: Windows 2000 computer (Professional, Server, or Advanced Server)

  - Computer B: Windows 2000 computer (Professional, Server, or Advanced Server)

Getting Down to Business

Step 1   Log on to Computer A using the built-in Administrator account and create a new folder named Products on your C drive.

Step 2   Right-click the folder and select Sharing. Share the folder as Accounting. Click the Permissions button. What is the default permission for the folder?

_____

_____

Step 3   Give the Read permission to the Everyone group.

Step 4   From Computer B, log on as a user and attempt to access the Products folder that you created on Computer A, by browsing to the folder using My Network Places. Were you able to access the folder? If so, why?

_____

_____

Step 5   What permissions are necessary to share a folder successfully?

_____

_____

Step 6   From Computer B, attempt to access the Products folder on Computer A by entering the UNC path of the Products folder at the Run command. Were you able to access the folder? If so, why?

_____

_____

Step 7   From Computer B, attempt to access the Products folder on Computer A by double-clicking My Network Places and selecting Map A Network Drive from the Tools menu.

Step 8   Browse to the Products folder on Computer A and click Finish.

Step 9   From Computer B, double-click the My Computer icon and verify that a mapped drive exists to the Products folder on Computer A.

 60 MINUTES

Lab 14.02: Understanding NTFS Permissions

You have been assigned the task of removing the default NTFS permissions on the Sales folder and assigning several different permissions to users on your network. The Sales group requires the Modify permission to the Sales folder while the user account Gregory requires Full Control of the Sales folder. The Administrators group should also have full control of the folder.

Learning Objectives

In this lab, you'll examine NTFS permissions. At the end of this lab, you will be able to

- Recognize NTFS permissions

- Assign NTFS permissions to users and groups

- Edit the default NTFS permissions

Lab Materials and Setup

For this lab exercise, you'll need

- Pencil and paper

- Windows 2000 operating system with an NTFS partition

- A Windows 2000 Global Security Group named Sales must exist before beginning the lab (no members are required)

- A Windows 2000 user account named Gregory must exist before beginning the lab

---

✔ **Tech Note**

The user account Gregory must be granted the user right to log on locally to the Windows 2000 computer. This can be accomplished with the Local Security Policy tool. Assign Gregory's account the right to log on locally in the User Rights subfolder of Local Policies.

Getting Down to Business

Step 1   Log on as Administrator to the Windows 2000 computer and create a folder named Sales on the NTFS partition.

Step 2   Right-click the folder and select Properties. The properties window should appear.

Step 3   Select the Security tab. View and list the NTFS permissions that are listed. What is the default NTFS permission for the Sales folder? Are the permissions shaded gray in color? If so, what does this signify?

_____

_____

Step 4   Remove the default permission from the Sales folder. Assign the Sales group the Modify permission to the Sales folder.

✖   **Warning**

You may get a warning message from Windows 2000 regarding removing default inherited permissions. Read the message carefully and follow the instructions to understand and successfully remove the default folder permissions.

Step 5   Assign Gregory the Full Control permission for the Sales folder.

Step 6   Assign the Administrators group Full Control permission for the Sales folder. Click OK to save your changes.

Step 7   Log off the Administrator account. Log on to the computer as Gregory. Attempt to access the Sales folder on the NTFS partition. Were you able to access the folder? Why or why not?

_____

_____

Step 8   Can you modify the folder while logged on as Gregory? Why would the Administrators group need to be granted access to the folder?

_____

_____

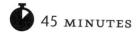 45 MINUTES

Lab 14.03: Sharing a Printer

You are the manager of a small pet supply store. You have just hired a new assistant and you want to ensure that he is able to send print jobs to the local printer you are about to install on your Windows 2000 computer. You do not want all others on the local network to be able to send their print jobs to your printer. You must install the printer and configure the permissions so that only you and your assistant are able to send print jobs to this printer.

Learning Objectives

In this lab, you'll examine the process of sharing a printer. At the end of this lab, you will be able to

- Share a printer

- Recognize the default printer permissions

- Assign appropriate permissions to the printer

Lab Materials and Setup

For this lab exercise, you'll need

- Pencil and paper

- A Windows 2000 computer (Professional, Server, or Advanced Server)

- A Windows 2000 user account named Assistant

Getting Down to Business

Step 1 From the Windows 2000 computer, double-click the Printers icon in the Control Panel.

Step 2 Double-click the Add Printer icon. The Add Printer Wizard appears. Click Next and proceed to add a Local Printer, using an available LPT port.

Step 3 Choose to install an HP2000C printer and ensure that it is the default printer.

Step 4 Share the printer as Manager. Do not enter a location or comment for the printer. Do not print a test page.

Step 5 Click Finish to allow Windows 2000 to install the correct drivers for the printer.

Step 6   Verify that the HP2000C appears in the Printers folder. How can you verify that it is the default printer? How can you verify that the printer is shared as Manager?

_____

_____

Step 7   Right-click the printer and select Properties from the menu. Select the Security tab.

Step 8   What are the default permissions for this printer?

_____

_____

Step 9   Remove the Everyone group from the permissions list and ensure that the Assistant account has the ability to print to the printer. Will this action still allow you to print to the printer you have installed? Who else is able to send print jobs to the printer? Why?

_____

_____

Lab Analysis

1. When sharing a folder over a network, is it necessary to set NTFS permissions on that folder if it is located on an NTFS partition?

_____

_____

2. Can a user on a Windows 2000 Professional computer share a folder over the network with another user?

_____

_____

3. How do UNIX/Linux permissions differ from Windows 2000 permissions?

_____

_____

✔ **Hint**

You may have to research on the Internet to answer this question, as we have not discussed UNIX/Linux permissions in this chapter.

4. What is the solution to the problem of mapped drives not reappearing after a user logs on?

_____

_____

5. What services must be installed on a Windows 2000 system to be able to share a printer? How does this compare with a Windows 98 system? How does it compare with a UNIX/ Linux system?

_____

_____

Key Term Quiz

Use the following vocabulary terms to complete the sentences below. Not all of the terms will be used.

File and Print Sharing

line printer (LPR)

line printer daemon (LPD)

Network File System (NFS)

NTFS permissions

persistent connection

share permissions

trustee rights

Universal Naming Convention (UNC)

Universal Resource Locator (URL)

1. User or group permissions on a shared folder are known as _____ in Novell NetWare.

2. The _____ command sends a print job to a network printer.

3. The format for specifying the location of resources on a network is called the _____.

4. Accessing a resource over the network in Windows 2000 requires an Administrator or Power User establishing _____ on the resource.

5. A mapped drive that reconnects at logon is known as a _____.

Lab Wrap-Up

Sharing resources and setting permissions may not be difficult, yet frequently we encounter sharing errors on our networks. With more advanced operating systems like Windows NT, Windows 2000, and Novell NetWare, combinations of permissions can lead to sharing errors and the dreaded "no access to resources" message.

You should now understand the process of sharing a folder and printer with Windows 2000. You should also recognize the default share and NTFS permissions for both types of resources. Remember, if you get into trouble with share errors, take your time and mentally review the steps when verifying that permissions have been granted or denied. Even the best administrators have been known to deny a user permission to a resource when they really wanted to grant permission!

Solutions

In this section, you'll find solutions to the lab exercises, the Lab Analysis questions, and the Key Term Quiz.

Lab 14.01 Solution

Step 1   Ensure that the Products folder is created as indicated in Figure 14-1.

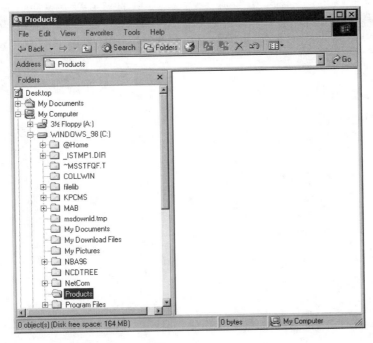

FIGURE 14-1 Products folder

Step 2   The default permission for all newly created folders is Full Control for the Everyone group.

Step 3   Ensure that you selected the Read permission as indicated in Figure 14-2.

Step 4   You should be able to access the folder as it was shared out successfully to the Everyone group, giving the Read permission to all users who can establish a connection to the folder. If you have problems accessing the folder, ensure that it is not a connectivity problem and ensure that you have successfully completed Step 3.

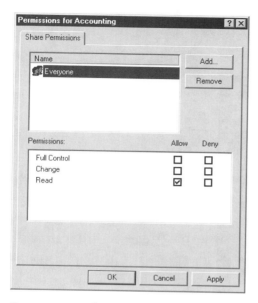

Figure 14-2 Sharing Products folder

Step 5 To share a folder successfully on a Windows 2000 computer, you must either be a member of the Administrators group or a member of the Power Users group.

Step 6 You should be able to access the folder by using the correct UNC path of *//server name/ share name*, as this is the correct location of the folder to which you have the Read permission.

Step 7 Ensure that you have selected to Map A Network Drive as indicated in Figure 14-3.

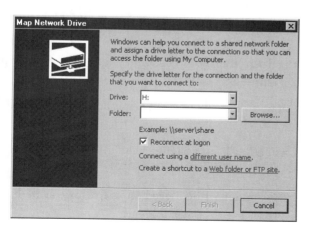

Figure 14-3 Map Network Drive

Step 8   Ensure that you have browsed to the Products folder and that the correct path appears as indicated in Figure 14-4.

Map Network Drive

Windows can help you connect to a shared network folder and assign a drive letter to the connection so that you can access the folder using My Computer.

Specify the drive letter for the connection and the folder that you want to connect to:

Drive: H:

Folder: .nwtraders.msft\products   Browse...

Example: \\server\share
☑ Reconnect at logon
Connect using a different user name.
Create a shortcut to a Web folder or FTP site.

< Back   Finish   Cancel

FIGURE 14-4   Products folder UNC path in Map Network Drive

Step 9   The mapped drive should appear in the My Computer window as if the folder were stored locally on the computer from which it is accessed.

Lab 14.02 Solution

Step 1   Ensure that the Sales folder is created on an NTFS partition as indicated in Figure 14-5.

Step 2   Ensure that you can view the properties of the Sales folder as shown in Figure 14-6.

Step 3   The default Sales folder permission is Full Control granted to the Everyone group. The permissions may be gray in color, indicating that they have been inherited from a parent object as shown in Figure 14-7.

Step 4   Ensure that you have removed the default permissions and assigned the Modify permission to the Sales group as indicated in Figure 14-8.

Step 5   Ensure that Gregory has been assigned the Full Control permission for the Sales folder as indicated in Figure 14-9.

Step 6   Ensure that the Administrators group has been assigned the Full Control permission for the Sales folder as indicated in Figure 14-10.

Step 7   You should be able to access the Sales folder while logged on as Gregory, as he has been assigned the appropriate permissions to access the Sales folder.

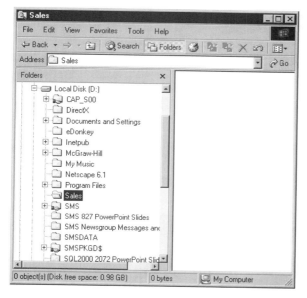

FIGURE 14-5 Sales folder

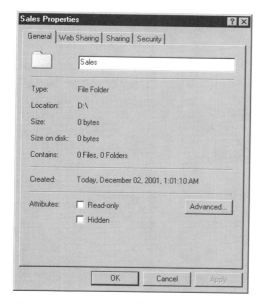

FIGURE 14-6 Sales folder properties

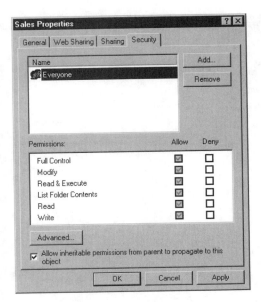

FIGURE 14-7 Default Sales folder permissions

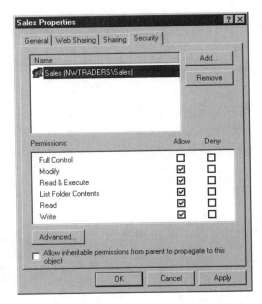

FIGURE 14-8 Sales group given Modify permission

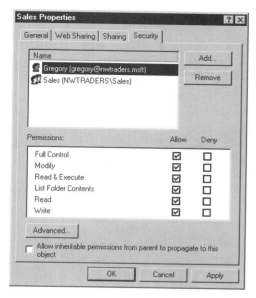

FIGURE 14-9 Gregory given Full Control permission

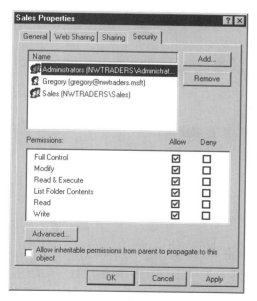

FIGURE 14-10 Administrators group given Full Control permission

Step 8 You should be able to modify the Sales folder while logged on as Gregory. The Administrators group should be given access to the folder, so in the case that they are not the owner/creator of the folder, they will still be able to access it and have Full Control over the folder and its contents.

Lab 14.03 Solution

Step 1   Ensure that the Printers folder is opened as indicated in Figure 14-11.

Step 2   Ensure that the Add Printer Wizard appears as indicated in Figure 14-12. Select Local Printer as shown in Figure 14-13.

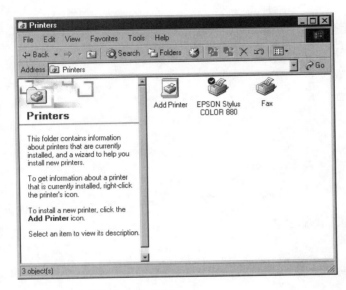

FIGURE 14-11 Printers folder

FIGURE 14-12 Add Printer Wizard

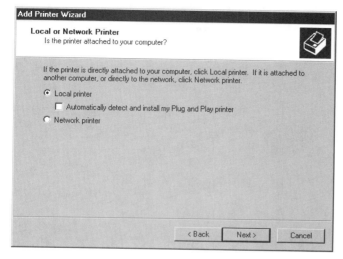

FIGURE 14-13 Add Local Printer

Step 3   Select the HP2000C printer from the list of printers as indicated in Figure 14-14. Ensure that the printer is the default printer, as indicated in Figure 14-15.

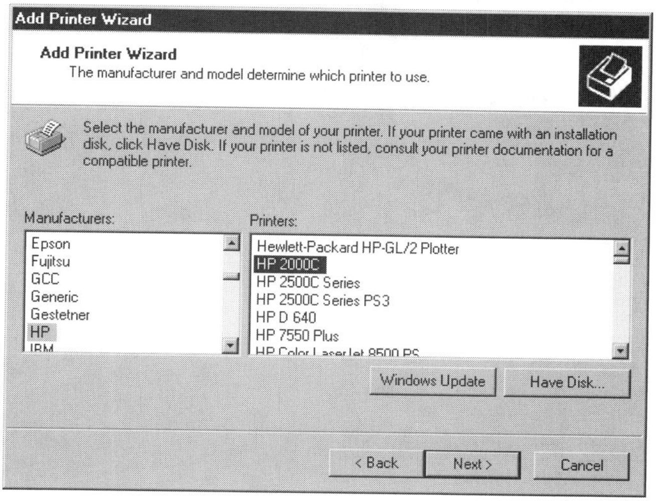

FIGURE 14-14 List of printers

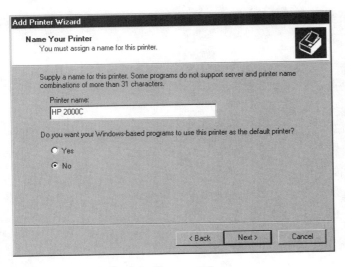

FIGURE 14-15 Default printer settings

Step 4   Ensure the printer is shared as Manager as indicated in Figure 14-16.

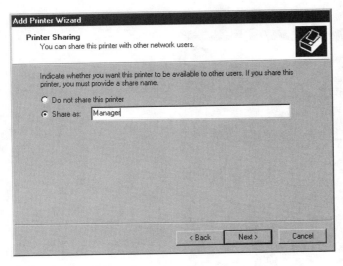

FIGURE 14-16 Shared as Manager

Step 5   Complete the process of adding a printer as shown in Figure 14-17.

FIGURE 14-17 Completing the Add Printer Wizard

Step 6 Ensure that the printer you added appears in the Printers folder, as shown in Figure 14-18.

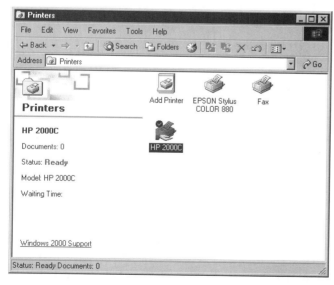

FIGURE 14-18 Printer appears as default printer in Printers folder

The checkmark next to the printer on the icon indicates that it is the default printer. The Sharing tab of the printer properties, as indicated in Figure 14-19, shows that the printer is shared with the name Manager.

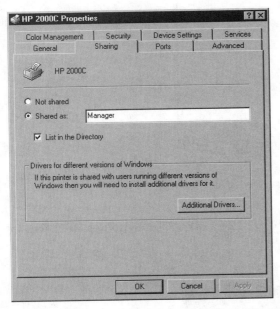

Figure 14-19 Sharing tab of the printer properties

Step 7   Ensure that the Security tab is selected, as indicated in Figure 14-20.

Step 8   The default permissions are

Administrators	Print, Manage Printers, Manage Documents
Creator Owner	Manage Documents
Everyone	Print
Printer Operators	Print, Manage Printers, Manage Documents
Server Operators	Print, Manage Printers, Manage Documents

Step 9   Ensure that the Everyone group is removed from the access list for the printer as indicated in Figure 14-21.

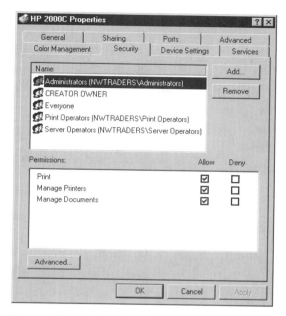

FIGURE 14-20 Security tab of the printer properties

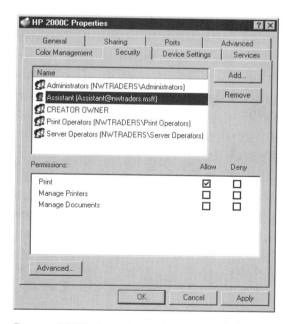

FIGURE 14-21 Security printer permissions assigned

This action will only allow you to print to the printer if you are a member of the Administrators, Printer Operators, or Server Operators group. They are the groups that are, by default, given permission to print to the printer. You must ensure that your account also has permission to print to the printer.

Answers to Lab Analysis

1. When sharing a folder over a network that is located on an NTFS partition, it is not necessary to assign NTFS permissions on the resource. NTFS permissions give administrators control over exactly what a user can or cannot do to a file or folder. They are not necessary when simply granting access to a shared resource over the network.

2. A user that has not been granted any special roles, such as a Power User or an Administrator, will not be able to share a resource over the network with another user. Only Power Users and members of the Administrators group have the ability to share resources in Windows 2000.

3. UNIX/Linux provides only three permissions:

Permission	User Ability
Read	Users can read files and folders, open files and subfolders, but cannot edit files
Write	Users can open and write to files
Execute	Users can execute files

4. If mapped drives are not reappearing after a user has logged on, these drives are not set up as persistent connections. To resolve the problem, when mapping a drive, you must select Reconnect At Logon, as indicated in Figure 14-22. Then, each time the user logs on, the mapped drives will reappear on his/her system and the connections will be made to the shared folders.

5. When sharing a printer on a Windows 2000 system, you must have the File and Printer Sharing for Microsoft Networks service installed. Windows 2000 installs this service automatically. Windows 98 also needs the File and Printer Sharing for Microsoft Networks service installed and the "I want to share my printers with others" check box checked. UNIX/Linux systems must have the line printer daemon (LPD) and line printer (LPR) service installed. The LPD service works on the server and runs on the systems sharing the printers. The LPR service runs on the systems wishing to access the shared printers.

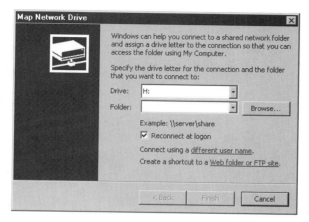

FIGURE 14-22 Reconnect At Logon

Answers to Key Term Quiz

1. trustee rights

2. line printer (LPR)

3. Universal Naming Convention (UNC)

4. share permissions

5. persistent connection

Chapter 15
Going Large with TCP/IP

Lab Exercises

Communicating with other clients and servers in a network environment may require going beyond the scope of your local company's network. To successfully communicate with other networks and the Internet, administrators use a variety of services and tools. In this chapter, we will look at Domain Name System (DNS), Dynamic Host Configuration Protocol (DHCP), and Windows Internet Naming Service (WINS). We will learn what function these services provide and how to configure them for use in our networks. We will also examine some of the tools that we can use to troubleshoot these services when we are confronted with errors.

 60 MINUTES

Lab 15.01: Examining Host Name Resolution

Tulloch Art Dealers wants to implement host name resolution on their network. They are unsure of how to do this and have hired you to assist them in their efforts. They wish to be able to connect to the Internet and access web sites through various web browsers. They require a solution that provides for minimal configuration by their administrators. You must present the various options for host name resolution and make a recommendation that will meet their requirements.

Learning Objectives

In this lab, you'll examine the options available for host name resolution. At the end of this lab, you will be able to

- Recognize the options for host name resolution

- List the advantages and disadvantages of each type of resolution

- Recommend a solution for a small company

Lab Materials and Setup

For this lab exercise, you'll need

- Pencil and paper
- Internet access

Getting Down to Business

Step 1 To connect to the web site www.yahoo.com, what options are available for host name resolution if you are unaware of the web site's IP address? List and define each name resolution option.

_____

_____

Step 2 Broadcasts are a form of name resolution. Would this option be available to Tulloch Art Dealers for host name resolution? Give reasons for your answer.

_____

_____

Step 3 What is the main disadvantage of using HOSTS files for name resolution in the Lab 15.01 scenario? If necessary, use the Internet to aid in your research.

_____

_____

Step 4 What are the advantages of implementing a DNS server for name resolution?

_____

_____

Step 5 Based on your knowledge, what solution would you recommend to Tulloch Art Dealers?

_____

_____

 60 MINUTES

Lab 15.02: Configuring a DHCP Server

You recently assumed the role of systems administrator for Cameron Industries. You have just installed the DHCP service on a domain controller and wish to configure a DHCP scope so that 30 users can obtain their IP addresses from the server. Your supervisor insists on having a static IP address. You must configure a DHCP scope that will accommodate your network requirements.

Learning Objectives

In this lab, you'll configure a DHCP server to dynamically provide IP addresses. At the end of this lab, you will be able to

- Authorize a DHCP server

- Create a DHCP scope

- Exclude an IP address from the scope

- Activate a DHCP scope

Lab Materials and Setup

For this lab exercise, you'll need

- Pencil and paper

- Windows 2000 domain controller with static IP address of 193.169.1.100

- Administrator account that is a member of the Enterprise Admins group

- DHCP service installed

- Internet access

Getting Down to Business

Step 1 Open the DHCP console from the Administrative Tools menu.

Step 2 Right-click DHCP and select Manage Authorized Servers.

Step 3   Click the Authorize button and enter the static IP address for your server. Click OK. Click Yes to confirm that this is the server you wish to authorize. Close the Manage Authorized Servers dialog box.

Step 4   In the DHCP console, right-click your server name and select New Scope from the menu.

Step 5   The New Scope Wizard appears. Click Next. Enter the name of your server in the Name field. Leave the Description field blank. Click Next.

Step 6   Enter the range of IP addresses as follows:

Start IP Address: **193.169.1.1**

End IP Address: **193.169.1.50**

Step 7   As you enter an IP address range, what happens to the Length and Subnet Mask fields?

_____

_____

Step 8   Click Next. Type **193.169.1.25** in the Start IP Address field to exclude this IP Address from the scope. Click Add. Click Next.

Step 9   On the Lease Duration page, set the duration of the lease to eight days. Click Next.

Step 10   Choose to configure DHCP options later. Click Next.

Step 11   Click Finish to complete and close the New Scope Wizard.

Step 12   The scope should appear in the DHCP console.

Step 13   Right-click on the server and select Activate from the menu to activate the scope.

 15 MINUTES

Lab 15.03: Understanding WINS

MacMaster Music is considering implementing Windows Internet Naming Service (WINS) on their small TCP/IP network. They are currently implementing LMHOSTS files on each computer and are finding that this is quite a tedious task to maintain. They have telephoned you to ask you a few questions about WINS.

Learning Objectives

In this lab, you'll examine WINS. At the end of this lab, you will be able to

- Understand the function of WINS
- Define the reasons to implement WINS on a network
- Troubleshoot WINS with the NBTSTAT command

Lab Materials and Setup

For this lab exercise, you'll need

- Pencil and paper
- Internet access

Getting Down to Business

Step 1 What is WINS used for on a network? Will WINS adequately replace the current method of using LMHOSTS files for NetBIOS name resolution?

Step 2 Define and describe two reasons for implementing WINS on a network. If necessary, use the Internet to aid in your research.

Step 3   What is required to configure a WINS client on a network? If necessary, use the Internet to aid in your research.

_____

_____

Step 4   What WINS configuration can be completed using the client Advanced TCP/IP Settings window shown in Figure 15-1?

_____

_____

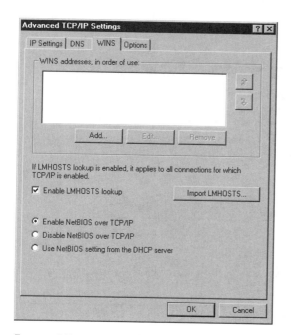

FIGURE 15-1 WINS tab of Advanced TCP/IP Settings

Step 5   What tool is available to troubleshoot WINS in the event of a problem? If necessary, use the Internet to aid in your research.

_____

_____

Lab Analysis

1. What are the two types of lookup zones that you can configure on a DNS server? Briefly describe each.

2. Using the DNS console in Figure 15-2, determine what types of records are shown in the Forward Lookup Zone. Briefly describe the function of each record.

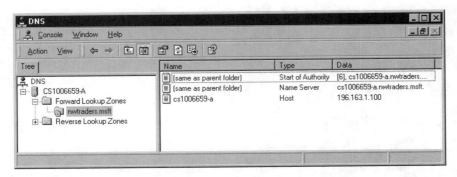

FIGURE 15-2 Forward Lookup Zone records

3. What type of IP address does a DHCP server use? Briefly describe the reason for your answer.

4. Can there be more than one WINS server on a network? Give reasons for your answer.

5. What does the ipconfig /flushdns command do as shown in Figure 15-3?

_____

_____

FIGURE 15-3 The ipconfig /flushdns command

Key Term Quiz

Use the following vocabulary terms to complete the sentences below. Not all of the terms will be used.

cached lookup

Dynamic Host Configuration Protocol (DHCP) scope

Forward Lookup Zones

NBTSTAT

NETSTAT

NET VIEW

NSLOOKUP

Reverse Lookup Zones

Start of Authority (SOA)

TRACERT

1. Authoritative DNS servers actually hold the IP addresses and names of systems for a particular domain or domains in _____.

2. _____ displays protocol statistics and current TCP/IP connections using NetBIOS over TCP/IP.

3. Running the _____ command will show you all the current connections to your system.

4. A _____ is the pool of IP addresses that a server may allocate to clients requesting IP addresses or other IP information like DNS server addresses.

5. A folder used by DNS that stores a list of all the IP addresses it has already resolved is called a _____.

Lab Wrap-Up

You have now seen how DNS, DHCP, and WINS can simplify the communication and administrative overhead on a network. DNS and WINS can provide accurate name resolution without the tedium of manual configuration. DHCP can accurately provide IP addresses to requesting clients, as well as reserve IP addresses. You will have to look long and hard to find a large network today that isn't implementing these essential services.

Solutions

In this section, you'll find solutions to the lab exercises, the Lab Analysis questions, and the Key Term Quiz.

Lab 15.01 Solution

Step 1   You can accomplish name resolution in two different ways: by using a HOSTS text file or by contacting a DNS server. A HOSTS file lists the names and addresses of machines on a network with their associated IP addresses. When an application needs to resolve a computer's host name, it can check the HOSTS file to determine the associated IP address and then make the connection to the remote computer. For example, the HOSTS file may have an entry for www.yahoo.com that resolves to the IP address of 192.168.1.1. Figure 15-4 shows a sample HOSTS file.

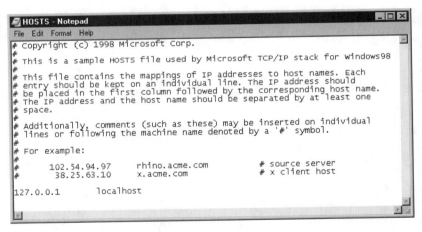

Figure 15-4 Sample HOSTS file

To resolve a name such as www.yahoo.com, the host can also contact a DNS server and request the IP address. The domain name service (DNS) on the server translates domain names to IP addresses and can pass this information back to the client's application requesting the name resolution.

Step 2   Broadcasts send requests to all computers on a network for an IP address that resolves to the host name that you supply. Broadcasts are not an option for name resolution in this scenario because routers do not forward broadcasts. To access the Internet and communicate beyond their internal network, Tulloch Art Dealers would need to find an alternate solution.

Step 3 The main disadvantage of using HOSTS files for name resolution is that it requires a great deal of overhead on the part of the administrator. A separate HOSTS file must exist on every computer that includes all the names and IP addresses of every computer that you wish to communicate with. As you can see, this would be quite daunting in the case of Tulloch Art Dealers, as they wish to communicate with other hosts by using the Web.

Step 4 There are two advantages to implementing DNS over implementing HOSTS files. The database of host names and IP addresses is centralized on the DNS server, allowing an administrator to add new entries all at once—resulting in less overhead on the part of the administrator. The database is also distributed. The DNS server simply has to know about the other DNS servers and how to contact them for the additional information that they need to resolve names for their clients.

Step 5 A DNS server added to the local network would provide for host name resolution with little administrative overhead. The users on the network could access the Internet through web browsers by typing in the domain names and the DNS server would take care of the name resolution either by searching through its own DNS cache or by contacting other DNS servers to retrieve the IP address.

Lab 15.02 Solution

Step 1 Ensure that the DHCP console is open, as indicated in Figure 15-5.

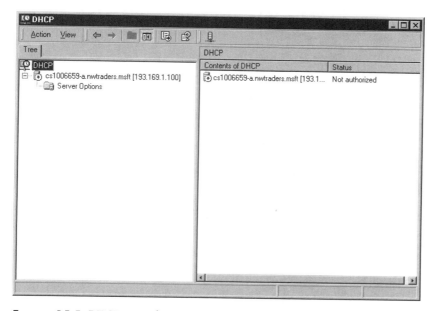

Figure 15-5 DHCP console

Step 2 Ensure that you have chosen Manage Authorized Servers, as shown in Figure 15-6.

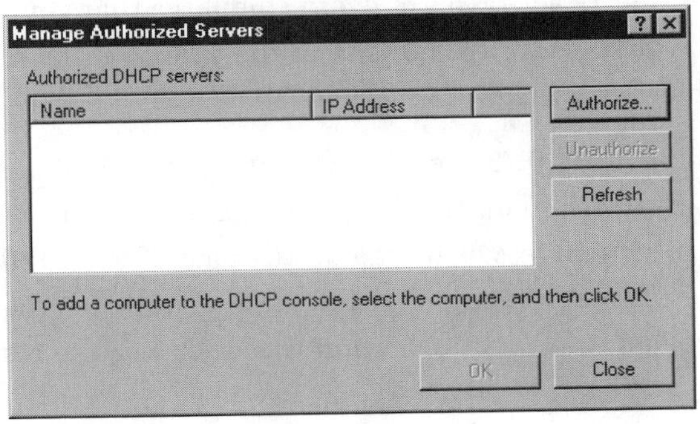

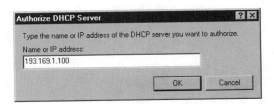

FIGURE 15-6 Manage Authorized Servers

Step 3 Choose to authorize your DHCP server by entering your IP address as indicated in Figure 15-7.

FIGURE 15-7 Authorize DHCP Server

Step 5 Ensure that the New Scope Wizard appears, as shown in Figure 15-8. Ensure that the name of your server is entered in the Name field, as shown in Figure 15-9.

Step 6 Ensure that the IP address ranges are entered, as shown in Figure 15-10.

Step 7 Windows 2000 automatically configures the subnet mask and bits for the designated range of IP addresses.

Step 8 Ensure that the IP address is entered as an exclusion, as shown in Figure 15-11.

FIGURE 15-8 New Scope Wizard

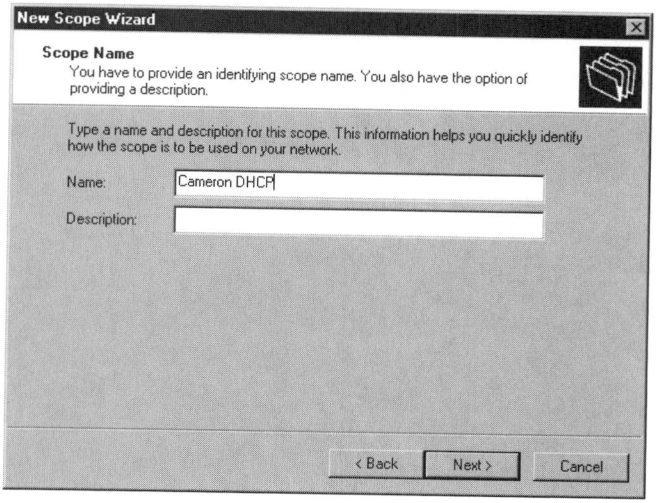

FIGURE 15-9 Name and Description of server in New Scope Wizard

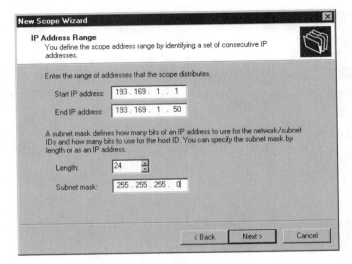

Figure 15-10 IP Address Range

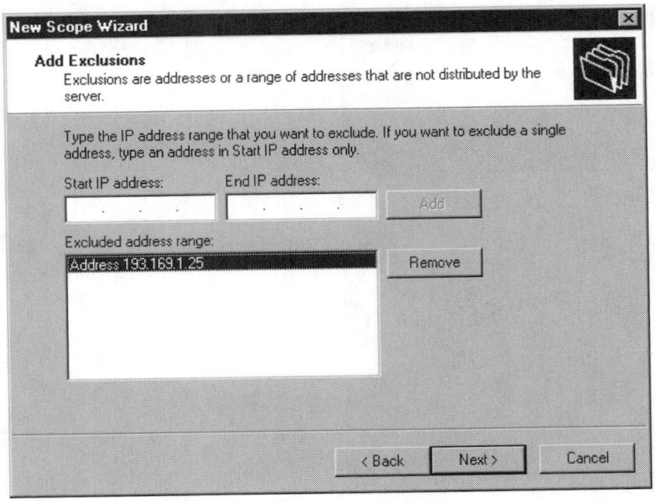

Figure 15-11 Add Exclusions

Step 9 Ensure that the lease duration is set to eight days, as shown in Figure 15-12.

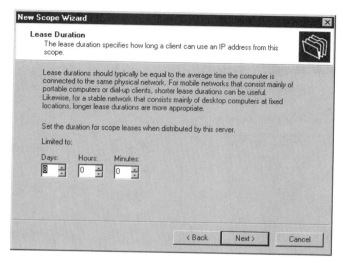

FIGURE 15-12 Lease Duration

Step 10 Choose to configure DHCP Options at a later date, as shown in Figure 15-13.

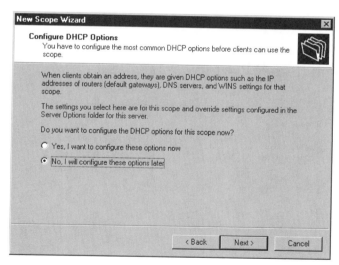

FIGURE 15-13 Configure DHCP Options

Step 11 Complete the addition of a new scope, as indicated in Figure 15-14.

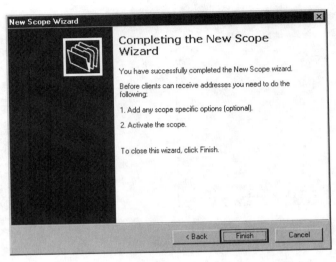

FIGURE 15-14 Completing the New Scope Wizard

Step 12 The newly created scope appears in the DHCP console, as shown in Figure 15-15.

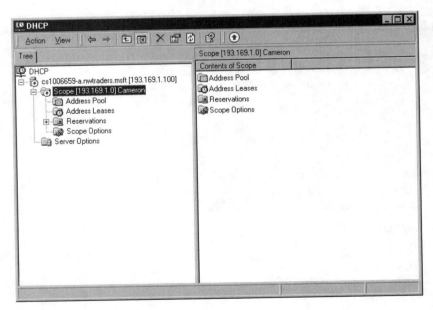

FIGURE 15-15 DHCP scope deactivated

Step 13   Ensure that the scope is activated, as shown in Figure 15-16.

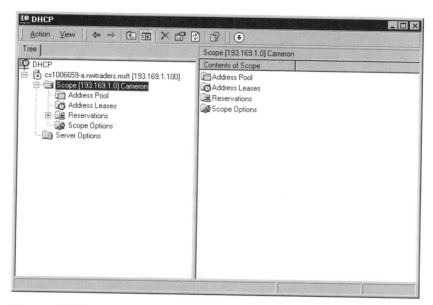

Figure 15-16 DHCP scope activated

Lab 15.03 Solution

Step 1   Windows Internet Naming Service (WINS) is a method of NetBIOS name resolution that determines the IP address associated with a particular network computer. WINS servers let NetBIOS hosts register their names with just the one server, eliminating the need for broadcasting. WINS can successfully replace the need for LMHOSTS files and eliminate the overhead involved in maintaining an accurate LHMOSTS file on every computer on the network.

Step 2   The first reason to use a WINS server on a network would be to reduce overhead from broadcasts and from implementing several LHMOSTS files. The second reason to implement WINS on a network would be to enable NetBIOS name resolution across routers through the use of WINS Relay Agents. WINS Relay Agents forward broadcasts for name resolution across routers to WINS servers on other networks. Normally, IP routers would not forward broadcasts.

Step 3   Every Windows client looks for the IP address of a WINS server automatically based on the settings that are defined in their LAN connection on startup. If it locates a WINS server, the client sends out a registration to the WINS server. A client must register its name with the WINS database if it is to function on the network.

If the client cannot find a WINS server, it will automatically start broadcasting. To configure a client for WINS you can add WINS information to DHCP, but this is only commonly seen if the client is using a static IP address; otherwise, no configuration on the client is necessary.

Step 4   The WINS tab of the Advanced TCP/IP Settings allows you to configure the IP address for the WINS server to which the client will connect. It also allows you to enable LMHOSTS lookup to search through a designated LMHOSTS file for name resolution. You can also choose to enable, disable, or configure a separate NetBIOS setting over TCP/IP. The default setting is to enable NetBIOS over TCP/IP, which is commonly used when implementing WINS.

Step 5   The NBTSTAT command displays protocol statistics and current connections using NetBIOS over TCP/IP. By running the command NBTSTAT –c, you can see the current NetBIOS name cache (IP addresses resolved to NetBIOS names) on a particular client computer. By using the NBTSTAT command, you can determine if the WINS server has displayed incorrect IP addresses to WINS clients.

Answers to Lab Analysis

1. The two types of zones that you can configure on a DNS server are indicated in the following list:

    Forward Lookup Zone   Enables a system to determine an IP address by knowing the Fully Qualified Domain Name

    Reverse Lookup Zone   Enables a system to determine a Fully Qualified Domain Name by knowing the IP address

2. The types of records found in the Forward Lookup Zone are shown in the following list:

    Start of Authority   Indicates the DNS server that either originally created it or is now the primary server for the zone.

    Names Server (NS)   Used to assign authority to specified servers in a DNS domain

    Host (A) record   Maps a domain name to an IP address

3. A static IP address is required for the DHCP server. For a DHCP server to successfully allocate IP addresses, it cannot automatically receive an IP address from another source.

4. It is recommended that you have more than one WINS server on a network to provide fault tolerance and to spread the workload. If one WINS server fails, the other can continue to resolve names to IP addresses. If you are implementing more than one WINS server, consider replicating each WINS database to the other WINS server so that each server can have an accurate list of hosts for name resolution.

5. The command ipconfig /flushdns will eliminate the DNS cache on the local computer. This command is frequently used before testing the DNS server so that you will have accurate results based on the current DNS server function and not based on old addresses maintained in the cache.

Answers to Key Term Quiz

1. Forward Lookup Zones

2. NBTSTAT

3. NETSTAT

4. Dynamic Host Configuration Protocol (DHCP) scope

5. cached lookup

Chapter 16

TCP/IP and the Internet

Lab Exercises

As companies choose to expand their networks to include connections to the Internet, several addressing and communication issues have to be considered. There are several tools and devices on the market that will aid network expansion dramatically and give administrators some well-deserved peace of mind.

In this chapter, we will examine routers and the advantages they bring to a network. We will also compare the function of Network Address Translation (NAT) products with proxy servers when protecting an internal network.

 60 MINUTES

Lab 16.01: Understanding Routers

TechTarget, Inc., has recently merged with another company and they are in the process of establishing connections from one Ethernet LAN to a second Ethernet LAN. They are unsure of whether to implement a router or a gateway to establish this communication. They have asked for your expertise in this matter and request that you make a recommendation for their network.

Learning Objectives

In this lab, you'll examine the functions and types of routers available. At the end of this lab, you will be able to

- Define the function of a router
- Recognize the different types of routers
- Define the function of a gateway
- Recommend a solution for TechTarget, Inc.

Lab Materials and Setup

For this lab exercise, you'll need

- Pencil and paper
- Internet access

Getting Down to Business

Step 1   Describe the functions of a router. Is the router always a separate hardware device or can a computer system be a router?

_____

_____

Step 2   What types of routers are popular for today's network environments? Research on the Internet to find three examples of routers used for small business environments. Record your results and the web site that provided the results in the space provided here.

_____

_____

Step 3   Describe the functions of a gateway. If necessary, use the Internet to assist in your research.

_____

_____

Step 4   Based on your knowledge of routers and gateways, which solution will satisfy the needs of TechTarget, Inc.?

_____

_____

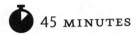 45 MINUTES

Lab 16.02: Comparing Proxy Servers and NAT

Hirsch Consulting is considering implementing a proxy server to improve performance for users accessing web sites. They also wish to have their internal IP addresses masked from external viewing. They are unsure if the proxy server will meet all their needs. They have asked you to present them with a solution that will satisfy their needs.

Learning Objectives

In this lab, you'll compare proxy servers with Network Address Translation (NAT). At the end of this lab, you will be able to

- Define the process of NAT

- Recognize the function of proxy servers

- Compare proxy servers and NAT

- Recommend an address translation solution for a small company

Lab Materials and Setup

- Pencil and paper

- Internet access

Getting Down to Business

Step 1 Describe the functions that a proxy server can provide on a network. If necessary, use the Internet to assist in your research.

_____

_____

Step 2 Describe the main purposes served by Network Address Translation. If necessary, use the Internet to assist in your research.

_____

_____

Step 3 How do NAT systems differ from proxy servers? If necessary, use the Internet to assist in your research.

_____

_____

Step 4 Should Hirsch Consulting implement a proxy server? Give reasons for your answer.

_____

_____

Lab Analysis

1. Based on your knowledge of proxy servers and NAT, list the advantages and disadvantages of each.

   _____

   _____

2. What is the difference between a gateway and a default gateway?

   _____

   _____

3. How can you see the routing table for an IP client? What information is presented in the routing table?

   _____

   _____

4. What command is available if you are having trouble connecting to the Internet or a remote network?

   _____

   _____

5. What is the function of the Telnet terminal emulation program? How can it help you when troubleshooting connection problems?

   _____

   _____

Key Term Quiz

Use the following vocabulary terms to complete the sentences below. Not all of the terms will be used.

File Transfer Protocol (FTP)

gateway

Hypertext Transfer Protocol (HTTP)

Internet Information Server (IIS)

Internet Message Access Protocol (IMAP)

Network Address Translation (NAT)

Post Office Protocol version 3 (POP3)

proxy server

router

Secure Sockets Layer (SSL)

Simple Mail Transfer Protocol (SMTP)

Telnet

1. _____ functions at the router level and protects an internal network by changing a system's IP address into another IP address before sending it out to an external network.

2. _____ can serve web pages, create FTP and newsgroup servers, and be administered remotely.

3. _____ is a message protocol that supports functions such as manipulation of server-based folders and filtering of messages from the server to client.

4. You can remotely administer a server through using the _____ program.

5. _____ is a protocol developed by Novell for transmitting private documents over the Internet.

Lab Wrap-Up

As you have now seen, there are many issues to consider when working with TCP/IP. Aside from configuring the protocol for IP address and subnet mask, and working with the DHCP and DNS services, you should also be concerned with address translation to protect your company's addressing from outside viewing. Through the implementation of proxy servers and NAT, you can accomplish this address masking and add extra security to your network.

Solutions

In this section, you'll find solutions to the lab exercises, the Lab Analysis questions, and the Key Term Quiz.

Lab 16.01 Solution

Step 1 A router directs incoming network protocol packets from one network to another based on its understanding of the networks that it is connected to. The router must be connected to at least two networks. Routers maintain a table of the available routes and their status and use this information along with distance of the route and the cost algorithms to determine the best route for a given packet. Routing is a function associated with the Network layer of the OSI model. Routers can be small or large devices or simply software that is added to a computer.

Step 2 Three examples of routers used for small business environments are listed here:

- The Linksys Instant Broadband EtherFast Cable/DSL Router connects a small group of PCs to a high-speed Broadband Internet connection or to an Ethernet backbone.

- The Cisco 1720 Access Router delivers an integrated solution for small branch offices and small and medium-sized businesses that want to deploy secure Internet/intranet and extranet access.

- The RouteFinder MTASR3 Ethernet Router (IP/IPX) provides secure and seamless LAN-to-LAN routing by connecting two or more LANs using a wide area network service.

Web sites will vary. These routers were found at chickshops.buybuddy.com/sleuth/15/1/10506/0//3/1/2/?index=1&pi=1.

Step 3 A gateway is a computer that lies at the intersection of two networks and routes traffic from one network to another, while keeping the two networks separated. A gateway connects two LANs that use different hardware, such as an Ethernet LAN to a Token Ring LAN. It also takes the network protocol packet, strips off the old protocol, and repackages it for the receiving network.

Step 4 TechTarget, Inc., needs to have a solution that provides communication between two Ethernet LANs; therefore, a gateway would not be an option as it is used to connect two or more different types of networks. A router that passes packets from one LAN to the next LAN would satisfy the requirements of TechTarget, Inc.

Lab 16.02 Solution

Step 1   Proxy servers can improve performance for users accessing web sites. They save the results of all web site requests on the server for a certain amount of time, returning the saved pages to subsequent users' requests rather than sending out requests for the same pages over and over again. Proxy servers can also be used to filter requests. Companies can use a proxy server to prevent their employees from accessing specific web sites. Proxy servers also masquerade IP addresses, allowing companies to have protected IP addresses internally, and separate public IP addresses for communicating with external networks.

Step 2   Network Address Translation (NAT) is an Internet standard that enables a network to use one set of IP addresses for internal traffic and a second set of addresses for external traffic. The NAT system, located where the LAN meets the Internet, makes all necessary IP address translations. You can read more about NAT at the web site www.vicomsoft.com/index.html?page=http://www.vicomsoft.com/knowledge/reference/nat.html*track=internal.

Step 3   NAT can sometimes be confused with proxy servers, but there are differences between them. NAT is transparent to the source and to destination computers but a proxy server is not transparent. The source computer knows that it is making a request to the proxy server based on the configuration at the source. The destination computer deals with the proxy server directly as if it were the source computer. Additionally, proxy servers work at the Transport layer of the OSI model or higher, while NAT is a Network layer protocol, making NAT systems faster.

Step 4   Hirsch Consulting is concerned with both address translation and the improvement in performance when accessing web sites; therefore a proxy server would meet their needs. It provides for both improved performance and address translation.

Answers to Lab Analysis

1.   Proxy server advantages include that they translate IP addresses, provide inexpensive solutions and optional WWW caching for better performance. The disadvantages of using a proxy server include the fact that all applications behind the proxy server must both support proxy services (SOCKS) and be configured to use the proxy server. The advantage of using NAT is that it is very configurable and provides address translation and no special application software is needed. The disadvantage of using NAT is that it requires a subnet from your ISP, which can be expensive. Another major problem with NAT is that once all of the free public IP addresses are used, any additional private users requesting Internet service are out of luck until a public NAT address becomes free.

2. A gateway connects two LANs that use different hardware. The default gateway is the IP address of the router interface that connects to your LAN.

3. By running the command route print at the client's command prompt, you can view the IP client's routing table. The table will consist of a list of active routes with IP address, subnet mask, gateway, and interface.

4. The PING command should be used on discovery of connection problems to the Internet or remote networks. This command checks to see if there are connectivity problems by pinging the remote host to get a reply. If there is a connectivity problem, you will either get a request timed out reply or a message indicating that the host was not found.

5. Telnet is a terminal emulation program for TCP/IP networks that allows you to connect to a server and run commands on that server as if you were sitting right in front of it. You can use Telnet to troubleshoot protocol connectivity and to remotely correct any errors, such as web site hacks, on a web server.

Answers to Key Term Quiz

1. Network Address Translation (NAT)

2. Internet Information Server (IIS)

3. Internet Message Access Protocol (IMAP)

4. Telnet

5. Secure Sockets Layer (SSL)

Chapter 17

Remote Connectivity

Lab Exercises

Remote access allows users to connect to a network from a remote location and work as if their computers were physically attached to the network. There are many different ways that a user can remotely connect to a network. In this chapter, we will look at the types of connections that you can make to a local area network (LAN), either through dial-up lines—Public Switched Telephone Network (PSTN) and Integrated Services Digital Network (ISDN)—or through high-speed connections such as asymmetric digital subscriber line (ADSL) and cable modems.

We will also plan for an implementation of a remote access server and clients in a company network and learn to configure a remote access server through the Routing and Remote Access component on a Windows 2000 Server.

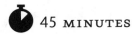 45 MINUTES

Lab 17.01: Comparing Hardware Types

Shannon is considering implementing a home office connection to access the Internet. She does not want to spend a lot of money yet she requires a high-speed solution so that she can upload and download images to the products page of her web site, *Shannon's Violins*. She has asked you to recommend a solution for her scenario. She has also asked you to provide her with some information on two WAN technologies that her parent company implements.

Learning Objectives

In this lab, you'll compare hardware types used for LAN and WAN connections. At the end of this lab, you will be able to

- Recognize dial-up connections to the Internet

- Recognize high-speed technologies
- Compare LAN and WAN hardware types

Lab Materials and Setup

For this lab exercise, you'll need

- Pencil and paper
- Internet access

Getting Down to Business

Step 1   Give a brief description of the common dial-up LAN connections PSTN and ISDN. If necessary, use the Internet to assist your research.

_____

_____

Step 2   Give a brief description of the high-speed Internet access technologies such as ADSL and cable modems. If necessary, use the Internet to assist your research.

_____

_____

Step 3   List the advantages and disadvantages associated with each LAN and WAN hardware type here:

Hardware Type	Advantages	Disadvantages
PSTN	_____	_____
ISDN	_____	_____
Cable Modem	_____	_____
X25	_____	_____
ATM	_____	_____

Step 4   Recommend an Internet connection solution for *Shannon's Violins* and give reasons for your recommendation.

_____

_____

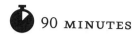 90 MINUTES

Lab 17.02: Planning for an Implementation of a Remote Access Server and Clients

Sanders Technology is an international training and consulting company running Windows 2000 domain controllers and servers and Windows 2000 Professional clients. Sanders Technology provides consulting and training services for small-to-moderate-sized companies throughout the United States and Europe. The main office for Sanders Technology is in Dallas, Texas. They also have regional locations in San Francisco, Boston, and London. Dallas is connected to San Francisco and Boston via dedicated T1 links. They also have a 56 Kb frame relay connection to London. These regional offices are remote offices, and each maintains and manages their own intranets. Occasionally, they send and receive data across these lines, but the offices usually operate independently of each other.

There are a total of 1,000 computers in use at the company: 400 are in Dallas, 250 in San Francisco, 250 in Boston, and 100 in London. The company has been growing steadily in all of these cities, with an anticipated growth of 200 percent over the next year alone.

Your goal is to ensure that the CIO has all the relevant information necessary to budget the installation and implementation of an efficient and cost-effective remote access solution for users who connect to their corporate networks from remote locations. Your plan is to install a remote access server at each company location. You have concluded that Windows 2000 Routing and Remote Access is the best solution for the company.

Learning Objectives

In this lab, you'll examine how to design a remote connectivity solution. At the end of this lab, you will be able to

- Determine a remote access connectivity solution

- Compare remote access protocols

- Plan client configuration for remote access

Lab Materials and Setup

For this lab exercise, you'll need

- Pencil and paper

- Internet access

Getting Down to Business

Step 1   What type of remote access connectivity would be best suited to Sanders Technology and why?

_____

_____

Step 2   Which remote access protocol would best be implemented with your choice of remote connectivity and why?

_____

_____

Step 3   What client operating systems are supported by your remote access connectivity solution for Sanders Technology?

_____

_____

Step 4   What is the major disadvantage with a dial-up connection directly to the remote access server at each company location of Sanders Technology?

_____

_____

 20 MINUTES

Lab 17.03: Configuring Remote Access on a Server

Perdicou Teapots needs a remote access solution for their remote clients. They are running several Windows 2000 servers and have decided to configure one of the servers as a remote access server. They have verified the compatibility of their hardware by using the Hardware Compatibility List (HCL), and then installed the hardware and configured all of the network protocols that dial-up users will use: TCP/IP, NWLink, NetBEUI, and AppleTalk. They have asked you to enable and configure remote access on the server.

Learning Objectives

In this lab, you'll configure and enable remote access through the Routing and Remote Access Server Setup Wizard of Windows 2000. At the end of this lab, you will be able to

- Configure a Windows 2000 server to allow remote access
- Use the Routing and Remote Access Server Setup Wizard

Lab Materials and Setup

For this lab exercise, you'll need

- Pencil and paper
- Computer with Windows 2000 Server or Advanced Server installed
- Computer with Routing and Remote Access component installed

Getting Down to Business

Step 1   Open Routing and Remote Access from the Administrative Tools menu. In the console tree, right-click the server name. Click Configure And Enable Routing And Remote Access.

Step 2   In the Routing and Remote Access Server Setup Wizard, click Next.

Step 3   On the Common Configurations page, select Remote Access Server. Click Next.

Step 4   On the Remote Client Protocols page, verify that you have all of the transport protocols that you want to use with remote access and then click Next.

Step 5   On the IP Address Assignment page, select Automatically to specify a range of IP addresses to assign to the dial-in clients. Click Next.

Step 6   On the Managing Multiple Remote Access Servers page, you can configure RADIUS (Remote Authentication Dial-In User Service) now or delay setup until later. Choose "No, I do not want to set up this server to use RADIUS now." Click Next.

Step 7   Click Finish to complete the wizard.

Once you have completed this process, you would normally verify that each dial-up client is allocated an appropriate IP address, DNS server address, IPX network address, NetBIOS name, or AppleTalk network when they are connected.

Lab Analysis

1. How does Internet Connection Sharing (ICS) affect a network connection to the Internet from a company LAN?

    _____

    _____

2. Aside from the X25 and ATM connections, T1 and T3 connections are popular in today's WAN environments. Briefly describe the characteristics of the T1 and T3 connections.

    _____

    _____

3. What are the advantages of using ISDN over PSTN?

    _____

    _____

4. What is a Channel Service Unit/Data Service Unit and how can it protect a company's router to a leased line from the telephone company?

    _____

    _____

5. What configuration is required on a remote access server to allow clients to connect?

    _____

    _____

Key Term Quiz

Use the following vocabulary terms to complete the sentences below. Not all of the terms will be used.

> asymmetric digital subscriber line (ADSL)
>
> Asynchronous Transfer Mode (ATM)
>
> Channel Service Unit/Data Service Unit (CSU/DSU)
>
> Integrated Services Digital Network (ISDN)
>
> Internet Connection Sharing (ICS)
>
> optical carriers (OCs)
>
> Point-to-Point Protocol (PPP)
>
> Point-to-Point Tunneling Protocol (PPTP)
>
> Public Switched Telephone Network (PSTN)
>
> Serial Line Internet Protocol (SLIP)
>
> Synchronous Optical Network (SONET)
>
> telephony

1. _____ is a standard for connecting fiber optic transmission systems.

2. _____ is a dial-up protocol that supports IPX and NetBEUI as well as IP.

3. With _____, users can dial into their corporate network via the Internet and send data that is encrypted.

4. _____ is the science of converting sound into electrical signals, moving them from one location to another and then converting them back into sounds.

5. _____ is a technology that allows multiple computers on a private network to connect to the public Internet via a single connection to the Internet.

Lab Wrap-Up

In this chapter, you learned the process that occurs when remote access clients attempt to connect to their company's LAN. You also learned the different methods of establishing remote access connections: dial-up connections and virtual private networks (VPNs). You were introduced to the Routing and Remote Access Service provided by Windows 2000 Server and the remote access protocols PPP, SLIP, and PPTP. You also learned about the advantages and disadvantages of using various LAN and WAN hardware types.

Solutions

In this section, you'll find solutions to the lab exercises, the Lab Analysis questions, and the Key Term Quiz.

Lab 17.01 Solution

Step 1 PSTN is the oldest, slowest, and most common phone connection based on twisted-pair copper wires carrying analog voice data. This technology uses RJ-11 connectors. Computers require modems to convert digital signals from the computer to the analog waveforms that travel across PSTN lines. PSTN phone lines take analog samples of sound 2400 times/second.

ISDN is a communications standard for sending voice, video, and data over digital telephone lines or telephone wires. It supports data transfer rates of 64 Kbps and can support two lines at once (called B channels), which allow you to use both lines to transfer data; this gives you data rates of 128 Kbps.

Step 2 ADSL is a fully digital, dedicated connection to the telephone system that provides download speeds up to 9 Mbps and upload speeds up to 1 Mbps over PSTN lines. Internet service providers must support ADSL. The most common ADSL installation includes an ADSL modem connected to a telephone jack and to a network interface card (NIC) in the computer.

A cable modem is a modem designed to operate over cable television lines. It is used to achieve extremely fast access to the Internet and provides throughput speeds of 256 Kbps to 2.5 Mbps. The most common cable modem installation consists of a cable modem connected to a cable outlet, and the cable modem connecting to a computer's NIC.

Step 3 The advantages and disadvantages of each hardware type are shown in the following list:

Hardware Type	Advantages	Disadvantages
PSTN	Universal availability; inexpensive modems; higher speeds available with DSL	Toll charges; low speeds unless using DSL; DSL is not available in all locations and requires expensive modems
ISDN	Faster than most PSTN connections; dedicated lines; wide availability in urban areas	Low speeds compared with DSL or cable modems; expensive adapters
Cable Modem	Very fast connections	Lower availability; expensive modems
X25	Secure, dedicated network	Distance between computers limited to length of cable or infrared sensor range
ATM	Fast transfer of data, video, and audio	Different transfer requirements for data and audio/video transmissions

Step 4 A cable-modem or ADSL connection would suit Shannon's needs. Both provide for fast uploading speed compared to PSTN and ISDN connections and even though they may be slightly more expensive, most Internet service providers today have packages available that make it affordable to home and small businesses.

Lab 17.02 Solution

Step 1 Sanders Technology should provide a virtual private network (VPN) solution. A VPN provides secure remote access through the Internet, rather than through direct dial-up connections. A VPN client uses an IP internetwork to create an encrypted, virtual, point-to-point connection with a VPN gateway on the private network. Typically, the user connects to the Internet through an Internet service provider (ISP), and then creates a VPN connection to the VPN gateway. By using the Internet in this way, Sanders Technology can reduce their long-distance telephone expenses and rely on existing infrastructure instead of managing their own infrastructures.

Step 2 Remote users from Sanders Technology can use the Point-to-Point Tunneling Protocol (PPTP) to connect to the VPN. PPTP is used to ensure that messages transmitted from one remote client to another are secure. With PPTP, users can access their corporate network (via the Internet) and send encrypted data.

Step 3 VPN clients using Windows 95, Windows 98, Windows NT 4.0, or Windows 2000 can connect to Windows 2000 Servers running Remote Routing and Access. Non-Microsoft VPN clients can connect to servers running Windows NT 4.0 or Windows 2000 provided they are using the VPN protocol PPTP with IPSec. All clients must be able to send TCP/IP packets over the network to the remote access servers.

Step 4 Remote access connections that dial up directly to the remote access server can produce long-distance telephone expenses. By using VPN connections instead of dial-up connections, traveling employees can dial the local ISP and then make a VPN connection back to the corporate network. This eliminates the long-distance charges or toll calls associated with a dial-up connection.

Lab 17.03 Solution

Step 1 Open Routing and Remote Access, as shown in Figure 17-1.

Step 2 The Routing and Remote Access Server Setup Wizard appears, as shown in Figure 17-2.

Step 3 Ensure that you are configuring a remote access server, as indicated in Figure 17-3.

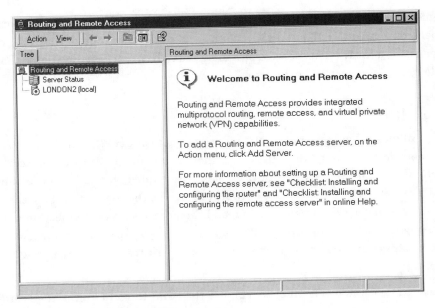

FIGURE 17-1 Routing and Remote Access

FIGURE 17-2 Routing and Remote Access Server Setup Wizard

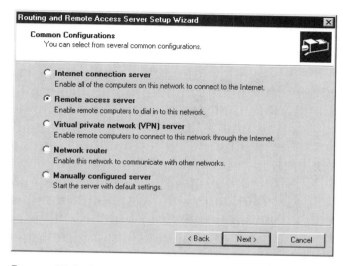

FIGURE 17-3 Common Configurations selecting Remote Access Server

Step 4 Ensure that the transport protocols appear in the list, as indicated in Figure 17-4.

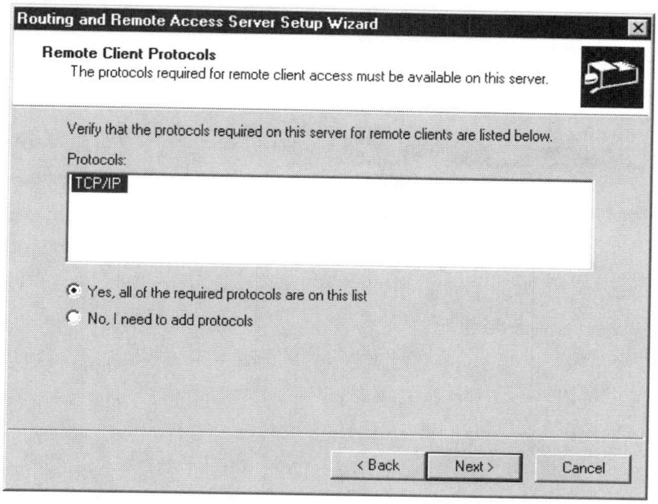

FIGURE 17-4 Remote Client Protocols

Step 5 Ensure that dial-in clients are assigned an IP address automatically, as indicated in Figure 17-5.

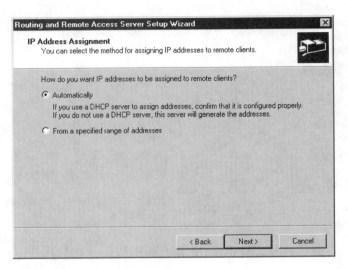

FIGURE 17-5 IP Address Assignment

Step 6 Ensure that you delay setup of RADIUS, as indicated in Figure 17-6.

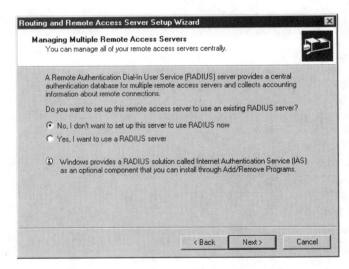

FIGURE 17-6 Managing Multiple Remote Access Servers

Step 7   Complete the Routing and Remote Access Server Setup Wizard, as shown in Figure 17-7.

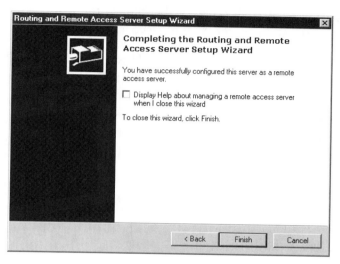

Figure 17-7 Completing the Routing and Remote Access Server Setup Wizard

Answers to Lab Analysis

1.   Internet Connection Sharing (ICS) allows more than one computer on a LAN to access the Internet simultaneously using a single Internet connection. You can actually connect an entire LAN to the Internet using a single public IP address. All of the other computers on the LAN can use private IP addresses, if needed.

2.   A T1 is a dedicated phone connection that can run at 1.544 Mbps. It can consist of 24 individual channels, each of which supports 64 Kbps and can transmit voice or data traffic. T1s are used by businesses connecting to the Internet. The T3 is a dedicated phone connection supporting a data rate of about 43 Mbps. It consists of 672 individual channels, each of which supports 64 Kbps. The T3 is mainly used by ISPs connecting to the Internet backbone.

3.   ISDN is faster than PSTN and connects more quickly. ISDN supports the ability to combine two B channels and carry data and voice information at 128 Kbps. ISDN also connects more quickly, eliminating the long modem conversations that can occur with PSTN connections.

4. A CSU/DSU is a piece of equipment that connects a leased line from the telephone company to a company's equipment (such as a router). It performs line encoding and conditioning functions. The CSU part of a CSU/DSU is designed to protect the T1 line and the user equipment from lightning strikes and other types of electrical interference.

5. You must configure the remote access server to recognize the client asking for access as a legitimate user for the client to connect successfully.

Answers to Key Term Quiz

1. Synchronous Optical Network (SONET)

2. Point-to-Point Protocol (PPP)

3. Point-to-Point Tunneling Protocol (PPTP)

4. telephony

5. Internet Connection Sharing (ICS)

Chapter 18

Protecting Your Network

Lab Exercises

Protecting networks from internal threats, such as unauthorized access and accidental data destruction, is as important as protecting networks from the external threats by hackers and viruses. We can use security policies and administrative control to protect against network failures from internal threats by our own users.

Protecting against external threats includes implementing firewalls, hiding IP addresses from external networks, and implementing authentication and encryption protocols.

In this chapter, we will look at protecting a network from external threats, compare authentication and encryption protocols, and configure a Windows 2000 local security policy.

 60 MINUTES

Lab 18.01: Protecting a Network from External Threats

Simpson & Chong Technologies has recently opened its business. They are allowing their users access to the Internet and are concerned that their network will be attacked and crippled by external threats from unknown Internet users. They have asked you to present them with a proposal for securing their network.

Learning Objectives

In this lab, you'll examine protecting a network from external threats. At the end of this lab, you will be able to

- Examine firewalls
- Describe port filtering
- Define packet filtering

Lab Materials and Setup

For this lab exercise, you'll need

- Pencil and paper
- Internet access

Getting Down to Business

Step 1 What is the function of a firewall and how can it help protect Simpson & Chong Technologies from external threats?

_____

_____

Step 2 How will port filtering help protect Simpson & Chong Technologies from attacks by hackers?

_____

_____

Step 3 Can a firewall include both Network Address Translation (NAT) and port filtering? Give reasons for your answer.

_____

_____

Step 4 What is packet filtering and how can it assist in protecting a network from external threats?

_____

_____

 60 MINUTES

Lab 18.02: Configuring a Windows 2000 Local Security Policy

You have been asked by your supervisor to configure a local security policy on a Windows 2000 file server. You will need to use the Local Security Policy console to do so. Your supervisor has given you a list of items that you are to configure.

Learning Objectives

In this lab, you'll configure a Windows 2000 local security policy. At the end of this lab, you will be able to

- Recognize the categories of security options

- Configure password policies

- Configure security options

- Configure and audit policy

Lab Materials and Setup

For this lab exercise, you'll need

- Computer with Windows 2000 Server or Advanced Server installed

- Ability to log on with Administrative privileges

Getting Down to Business

Step 1   From the Administrative Tools menu, select Local Security Policy. The Local Security Settings console appears. Expand the Account Policies container. Select the Password Policy container.

Step 2   Configure a password policy that has the following settings:

- Enforce Password History—15 passwords remembered

- Maximum Password Age—21 days

- Minimum Password Age—0 days

- Minimum Password Length—8 characters

You must double-click each policy object to obtain the configuration settings for the object.

Step 3 Expand the Local Policies container. Select the Audit Policy container.

Step 4 Configure an audit policy that has the following settings:

- Audit Account Logon Events—Success and Failure
- Audit Logon Events—Success, Failure
- Audit Object Access—Success, Failure
- Audit Privilege Use—Failure

Step 5 Select the Security Options container.

Step 6 Configure a user rights assignment policy that has the following settings:

- Do not display last user name in logon screen—Enabled
- Prompt user to change password before expiration—12 days

  Close the Local Security Settings console.

 45 MINUTES

Lab 18.03: Comparing Authentication and Encryption Protocols

Your friend Susan is studying for the Network+ exam and has called asking you to explain the differences between some of the popular authentication and encryption protocols. You are a security expert and want to provide Susan with a brief description of each protocol so she will understand the functions they provide.

Learning Objectives

In this lab, you'll compare authentication and encryption protocols. At the end of this lab, you will be able to

- Define and describe the PAP, CHAP, and MS-CHAP protocols
- Compare the features of the PPTP and L2TP protocols
- Understand IP Security (IPSec)

Lab Materials and Setup

For this lab exercise, you'll need

- Pencil and paper
- Internet access

Getting Down to Business

Step 1   Give a brief description of the PAP protocol.

_____

_____

Step 2   Give a brief description of the CHAP protocol.

_____

_____

Step 3 Give a brief description of the MS-CHAP protocol.

_____

_____

Step 4 List the differences between the PPTP and L2TP protocols in the areas listed here. Use the Internet to assist you in your research.

Areas of Difference	PPTP	L2TP
Connectivity	_____	_____
Header Compression	_____	_____
Authentication	_____	_____
Encryption	_____	_____

Step 5 What is IP Security (IPSec) and how can it help network security?

_____

_____

Lab Analysis

1. What advice can you give users that will help them keep their passwords secure? List five tips that will help to prevent other users from guessing or accessing their passwords.

_____

_____

_____

_____

_____

2. Why should you audit both logon successes and failures when establishing an audit policy?

_____

_____

3. What are some commonly used local policies that you can enable on a Windows 2000 system? List and define five policies.

_____

_____

_____

_____

_____

4. What encryption protocols are most popular when implementing virtual private networks (VPNs)?

_____

_____

5. What is HTTPS and how can it help you when adding security to your network?

_____

_____

Key Term Quiz

Use the following vocabulary terms to complete the sentences below. Not all of the terms will be used.

Challenge Handshake Authentication Protocol (CHAP)

demilitarized zone (DMZ)

group policies

IP Security (IPSec)

Layer Two Tunneling Protocol (L2TP)

Microsoft Challenge Handshake Authentication Protocol (MS-CHAP)

packet filters

Password Authentication Protocol (PAP)

1. Microsoft's transparent encryption method between the server and the client is known as _____.

2. A _____ is a lightly protected or unprotected network positioned between your firewall and the Internet.

3. _____ can be applied to a Windows 2000 computer to control hundreds of security parameters.

4. _____ will block any incoming or outgoing packet from a particular IP address or range of IP addresses.

5. _____ is an encryption protocol often seen on dedicated virtual private network (VPN) systems.

Lab Wrap-Up

As you have learned, there are many options available when choosing to implement security for your network, from firewalls to protocols to policies. It is extremely important that you choose the strictest means of enforcement while not limiting your own user access to resources. It is not often that you hear a network administrator say, "I wish I hadn't secured my network so well." So remember, the more steps you take to protect your network from both internal and external threats, the more secure your network will be.

Solutions

In this section, you'll find solutions to the lab exercises, the Lab Analysis questions, and the Key Term Quiz.

Lab 18.01 Solution

Step 1   A firewall is a system, whether software or hardware, that is designed to prevent unauthorized access to or from a private network. All messages entering or leaving the local network pass through the firewall and are examined. The firewall blocks those messages that do not meet the security criteria specified by the company network. Firewalls are often used to protect a network from external threats from the Internet. Simpson & Chong Technologies can benefit from a firewall as they are implementing Internet access for their users.

Step 2   Port filtering is the process of preventing the passage of IP packets through any ports other than the ones described by the system administrator. Port filtering requires configuration by the administrator but results in a very effective means of providing security. Port filtering can be installed on a firewall and is often implemented on routers and gateways. Simpson & Chong Technologies can benefit by port filtering because most of the common ports known by hackers to access a network can be closed or reconfigured so that they deny the hackers access.

Step 3   A firewall can include both Network Address Translation (NAT) and port filtering; however, it requires some additional configuration. Most gateway routers come with both NAT and port filtering.

Step 4   Packet filtering will block any incoming or outgoing packets from a particular IP address or range of IP addresses. So, if you know of a certain IP address that has been responsible for threats in the past, you can block all packets from that address to minimize your risk of being infiltrated. Firewalls can implement packet filtering and stop denial of service attacks that can bring down a server.

Lab 18.02 Solution

Step 1   Figure 18-1 shows the default password policy settings.

Step 2   Ensure that a password policy is defined with the settings shown in Figure 18-2.

Step 3   Figure 18-3 shows the default audit policy settings.

Step 4   Ensure that an audit policy is defined with the settings shown in Figure 18-4.

Step 5   Figure 18-5 shows the default security options settings.

Step 6   Ensure that the security options are configured as shown in Figure 18-6.

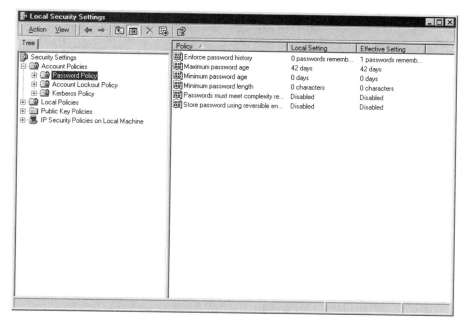

FIGURE 18-1 Password Policy default settings

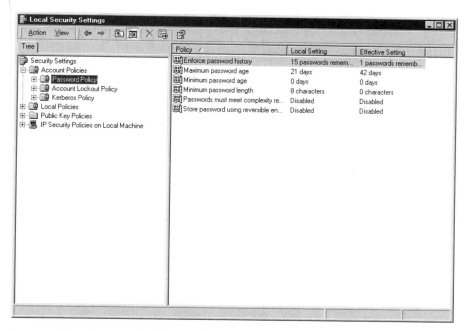

FIGURE 18-2 Password Policy configured

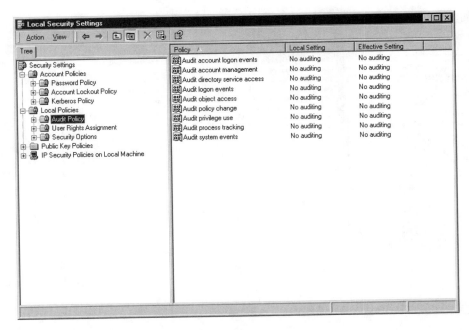

FIGURE 18-3 Audit Policy default settings

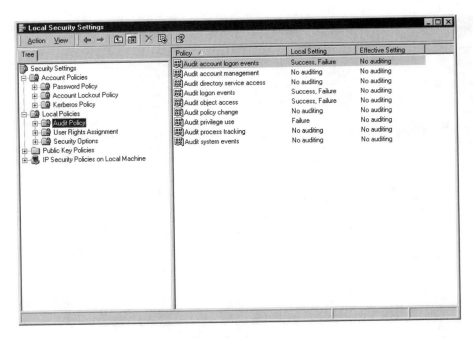

FIGURE 18-4 Audit Policy configured

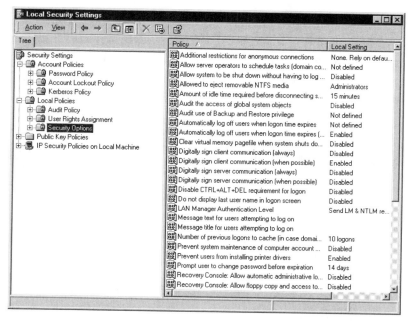

FIGURE 18-5 Security Options default settings

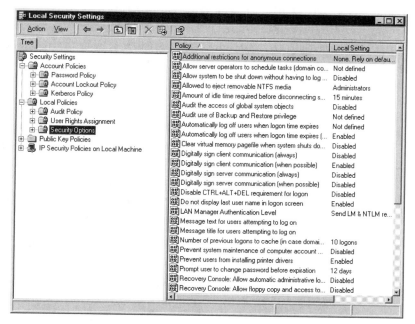

FIGURE 18-6 Security Options configured

Lab 18.03 Solution

Step 1 The Password Authentication Protocol (PAP) uses clear-text passwords, providing little protection against unauthorized access. If the passwords match, the server grants access to the remote access client. This protocol is normally only used as a last resort, as it provides very little security.

Step 2 The Challenge Handshake Authentication Protocol (CHAP) is a challenge-response authentication protocol. CHAP uses the industry-standard MD5 one-way encryption scheme to encrypt the response, providing a high level of protection against unauthorized access. The authentication process works as follows:

1. The remote access server sends a challenge, consisting of a session identifier and an arbitrary challenge string, to the remote access client.

2. The remote access client sends a response that contains the user name and a one-way encryption of the challenge string, the session identifier, and the password.

3. The remote access server checks the response and, if valid, allows the connection.

This process makes sure that the password is never sent across the network, therefore ensuring high-level security.

Step 3 Microsoft Challenge Handshake Authentication Protocol (MS-CHAP) is a one-way, encrypted password authentication protocol. If the server uses MS-CHAP as the authentication protocol, it can use Microsoft Point-to-Point Encryption (MPPE) to encrypt data to the client or server. On a remote access server running Windows 2000, MS-CHAP is enabled by default.

Step 4

Areas of Difference	PPTP	L2TP
Connectivity	Requires an IP-based inter-network and requires greater protocol overhead	Performs over a wide range of WAN connection media such as IP or frame relay, requiring only that the tunnel media provide packet-oriented, point-to-point connectivity
Header Compression	Does not support header compression; headers are always six bytes	Supports header compression; when enabled, operates with headers of four bytes

Areas of Difference	PPTP	L2TP
Authentication	Does not support tunnel authentication	Supports tunnel authentication; Internet Protocol Security (IPSec) provides computer-level authentication, in addition to data encryption
Encryption	Uses the Microsoft Point-to-Point Encryption (MPPE) algorithm	Provides a secure host-to-host tunnel by cooperating with other encryption technologies, such as IPSec

Step 5   IPSec is a set of protocols that supports the secure exchange of packets at the IP layer. IPSec supports two encryption modes: transport and tunnel. Transport mode encrypts only the data portion of each packet, and not the header. Tunnel mode encrypts both the header and the data portion and therefore is more secure. IPSec-compliant devices also decrypt each packet on receipt.

A big advantage of IPSec is that security can be handled without requiring changes to individual user computers. For IPSec to work, the sending and receiving devices must share a public key. For more information on IPSec you can refer to the following web site: www.ietf.org/ids.by.wg/ipsec.html.

Answers to Lab Analysis

1. Users should

    a) Never use obvious passwords such as a pet name, spouse name, etc.

    b) Use both numbers and letters in their passwords.

    c) Use both uppercase and lowercase letters.

    d) Ensure that they never tell anyone their password.

    e) Ensure that they don't write their password down in an unsecured location.

2. You should audit both logon successes and failures to determine if unauthorized users are attempting to access your network and if access has been granted successfully to these unauthorized users.

3. Several commonly used local policies are

    Log on locally   This policy defines who may log on to the system locally.

    Shut down system   This policy defines who may shut down the system.

Minimum password length   This policy forces a minimum password length.

Account lockout threshold   This policy sets the maximum number of logon attempts a person can make before they are locked out of the account.

Printer browsing   This policy allows users to browse for printers on the network, as opposed to using only assigned printers.

4.   Layer Two Tunneling Protocol (L2TP) and Point-to-Point Tunneling Protocol (PPTP) are two popular protocols used when employing encryption on virtual private networks.

5.   HTTPS is Secure Hypertext Transfer Protocol, a web protocol that is designed to transmit individual messages securely.

Answers to Key Term Quiz

1.   IP Security (IPSec)

2.   demilitarized zone (DMZ)

3.   group policies

4.   packet filters

5.   Layer Two Tunneling Protocol (L2TP)

Chapter 19

Interconnecting NOSs

Lab Exercise

Quite often large company networks will have computers running several different network operating systems (NOSs). It is imperative that administrators understand what tools allow these different operating systems to communicate with each other. They should also understand the limitations of the tools and how to best implement them to achieve effective communication.

In this chapter, we will learn how to establish communication between two networks that have several different network operating systems. We will identify the tools, services, and protocols that are needed on the systems, and recommend a communication solution for a two-company merger.

 60 MINUTES

Lab 19.01: Interconnecting Different NOSs

Primetime News has just merged with FIXT Cable News and they have asked you to recommend a solution for interconnecting their different network operating systems so that they can communicate. Primetime News is currently implementing a Microsoft Windows 2000 environment with 15 Windows 2000 Advanced Server servers and 2000 Windows 2000 Professional clients. They are running the TCP/IP protocol exclusively. FIXT Cable News is running 6 Novell NetWare servers with 500 Windows 98 clients. They are running the IPX/SPX and TCP/IP protocols. They require a solution that is simple, quick, and provides a smooth transition.

Learning Objectives

In this lab, you'll examine connecting different network operating systems. At the end of this lab, you will be able to

- Identify tools, services, and protocols for interconnection of the NOSs

- Define and describe connection services
- Recommend a connection solution

Lab Materials and Setup

For this lab exercise, you'll need

- Pencil and paper
- Internet access

Getting Down to Business

Step 1 Indicate the tools, services, or protocols necessary to provide communication between the different network operating systems and the associated clients. Clients and servers of the same operating system are not applicable for this exercise.

Network Operating System	Windows Client	Macintosh Client	Linux Client
Connecting to Windows 9x systems	N/A	_____	_____
Connecting to Microsoft Windows NT/2000 systems	N/A	_____	_____
Connecting to Novell NetWare systems	_____	_____	_____
Connecting to Macintosh systems	_____	N/A	_____
Connecting to Linux systems	_____	_____	N/A

Step 2 What recommendation would you make to simplify communication between the two news networks? Indicate what services or protocols they need to install on the servers and clients.

_____

_____

Step 3 If Primetime News decided to implement an additional UNIX server, how would this affect communication and what additional tools or services would you recommend they implement?

_____

_____

Lab Analysis

1. What file system protocols must be installed on a Windows 9x system for it to share resources?

   _____

   _____

2. What services are necessary on a Windows 2000 Professional client to connect to a Windows 2000 Server?

   _____

   _____

3. What configuration is necessary to connect a Macintosh client to a Windows 2000 Server and enable the client to access a shared folder?

   _____

   _____

4. What is the function of the DAVE program?

   _____

   _____

5. What program can you use to share resources on a Macintosh server to connected Windows or Linux systems?

   _____

   _____

Key Term Quiz

Use the following vocabulary terms to complete the sentences below. Not all of the terms will be used.

DAVE

File Sharing for Macintosh

Gateway Services for NetWare (GSNW)

Microsoft Windows Services for UNIX (MWSU)

multi-protocol routers

Samba

Services for UNIX (SFU)

Virtual Network Computing (VNC)

1. Connecting Linux systems to Windows 9x systems for native access to shared folders requires you to run a program called _____.

2. _____ is a service for Windows NT and 2000 servers that can be installed on these servers to enable them to directly access file and print resources on Novell NetWare servers.

3. _____ can translate IP packets into IPX packets.

4. Microsoft has an add-on product called _____ that enables Windows NT and 2000 systems to share their resources with Linux clients.

5. An excellent third-party terminal emulator that runs on several client operating systems and from a web browser is the _____ product.

Lab Wrap-Up

You should now be able to identify some of the various third-party tools that are available on the market today to aid in communication between different network operating systems. You should also be able to recognize the protocols and services that need to be installed on both clients and servers to provide communication between the operating systems.

Solution

In this section, you'll find solutions to the lab exercises, the Lab Analysis questions, and the Key Term Quiz.

Lab 19.01 Solution

Step 1   The tools, services, or protocols necessary to provide communication between the different network operating systems and the associated clients are listed here:

Network Operating System	Windows Client	Macintosh Client	Linux Client
Connecting to Windows 9x systems	N/A	Third-party tool MACLAN and TCP/IP protocol on client	Samba program on Linux client or NFS protocol and third-party product (OMNI NFS) on Windows 9x server
Connecting to Microsoft Windows NT/2000 systems	N/A	File Sharing for Microsoft and AppleTalk protocol installed on server *and* Windows accounts for Macintosh clients on server	Services for UNIX (SFU) and TCP/IP protocol installed on server
Connecting to Novell NetWare systems	Windows client for NetWare or Gateway Services for NetWare running on an NT/ 2000 server that a Microsoft client connects to	Macintosh client for NetWare	Linux client for NetWare
Connecting to Macintosh systems	AppleShareIP program on server or DAVE program on server	N/A	NFS program on server or NFS tools on Linux client

Network Operating System	Windows Client	Macintosh Client	Linux Client
Connecting to Linux systems	Samba program on server *or* Microsoft Windows Services for UNIX on NT/ 2000 systems *and* third-party NFS client (OMNI NFS) program on Windows 9x clients	NFS support on client and server *or* Nettalk program on client with optional GUI AppleTalk Configurator	N/A

Step 2 FIXT Cable News already has Windows 9x clients communicating with NetWare servers; therefore, these clients must be running the Windows Client for NetWare and either the TCP/IP or the IPX/SPX (compatible) protocols.

For the Windows 2000 Professional clients to successfully communicate with the NetWare servers, they must also either install the Windows Client for NetWare or choose to use their Windows 2000 Servers to connect to the NetWare servers indirectly. If they choose to implement a Windows 2000 Server as a gateway, then they must install the Gateway Services for NetWare service on the Windows 2000 Server. This would allow all Microsoft clients in Primetime News to connect to their same Windows 2000 Servers and access the NetWare server as if it were another Windows server. The Windows 2000 Professional clients must also run the IPX/SPX (compatible) protocol in this scenario. The Gateway Services for NetWare service installs the IPX/SPX protocol on the server.

For the Windows 9x clients to successfully communicate with the Windows 2000 Servers, they must have the Client for Microsoft Networks installed on their clients, as well as the TCP/IP protocol.

Step 3 If you add a UNIX server to the Primetime News network, you must ensure that there is some way for the Windows 98 and 2000 Professional clients to communicate with the system. Samba can be added and configured on the UNIX system. This would make all the resources on the UNIX server visible for the Windows clients.

Another solution would be to install the Microsoft Windows Service for UNIX (MWSU) group of services. This group includes the Gateway Services for UNIX that can enable the Windows 2000 Server to act as a gateway between Windows 98 and 2000 Professional clients and the UNIX server. All clients and servers should also run the TCP/IP protocol.

Answers to Lab Analysis

1. Network File System (NFS) can be installed on a Windows 9x server system and it will enable the system to share its resources.

2. The Client for Microsoft Networks is necessary on a Windows 2000 Professional client to connect to a Windows 2000 Server.

3. File Sharing for Macintosh must be installed on the Macintosh client and the share that is created on the Windows 2000 server must specify that it is intended to be shared by a Macintosh client. The Macintosh client will also need to have a valid user account on the Windows 2000 server.

4. DAVE is a program that enables small networks of Windows clients to access shared folders and printers on Macintosh servers. DAVE runs on the Macintosh server and does not require the Windows clients to run any additional software to connect to the Macintosh server. DAVE also enables Macintosh clients to access shared folders on Windows systems.

5. The AppleShare IP program enables a Macintosh server to share its resources with Windows and Linux systems. The DAVE program, as you have learned, can also be used on the Macintosh server.

Answers to Key Term Quiz

1. Samba

2. Gateway Services for NetWare (GSNW)

3. multi-protocol routers

4. Services for UNIX (SFU)

5. Virtual Network Computing (VNC)

Chapter 20
The Perfect Server

Lab Exercises

Maintaining a perfect server may be an impossible task, especially when it comes to network connectivity, data protection, speed, and reliability. However, there are methods and options that you can implement on your server that will prevent you from losing your data even when a disk fails. There are also many things you should know about how devices on your computer access other devices, including the four main system resources that are assigned to devices.

In this chapter, we will examine the system resources that are available for devices on a personal computer. We will also compare the fault tolerance solutions that Redundant Array of Independent Disks (RAID) provide and recommend a solution for a large company.

 60 MINUTES

Lab 20.01: Examining System Resources

You have just been hired as a junior technician and your first task is to determine whether there are any device conflicts on all of the Windows 2000 computers in the company. You determine that you will use the Computer Management console that Windows 2000 provides to help you discover any conflicts and examine the system resources that the company uses.

Learning Objectives

In this lab, you'll examine and compare the types of system resources that are available for your computer's devices. At the end of this lab, you will be able to

- Recognize the four types of system resources
- Describe the functions of the system resources
- View and analyze your computer's system resources

Lab Materials and Setup

For this lab exercise, you'll need

- Pencil and paper

- Internet access

- Windows 2000 Server or Advanced Server

Getting Down to Business

Step 1   From your Windows 2000 computer, open the Computer Management console from the Administrative Tools menu. In the left pane, expand the System Information object. Expand the Hardware Resources object. What folders signify the system resources on your computer? List each resource.

_____

_____

Step 2   Select the IRQ folder. List the IRQ numbers and the devices that are using each one for your computer. What are IRQs? Why are some IRQs not listed? What is the range of IRQ numbers available for use?

_____

_____

Step 3   Select the DMA folder. What DMA channels are your computer's devices currently using? How many DMA channels are available for use on a personal computer? Which DMA channels are reserved and for what devices?

_____

_____

Step 4   Select the I/O folder. View the devices listed. What is the definition of an I/O port?

_____

_____

Step 5 Select the Memory folder. View the devices listed. What is a memory address used for?

_____

_____

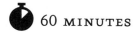 60 MINUTES

Lab 20.02: Comparing Fault Tolerance Solutions

OV Investments has asked you to recommend a fault tolerance solution for their company. They need to implement a solution that will ensure that they will not lose any data through the loss of a single disk drive. Their requirements are for fast writing of data to the disks. They do not have any financial restrictions and therefore can implement any solution, regardless of expense.

Learning Objectives

In this lab, you'll compare various fault tolerance solutions and recommend a fault tolerance solution for a large company. At the end of this lab, you will be able to

- Identify fault tolerance solutions

- Recognize the hardware required for each solution

- Recommend a fault tolerance solution for a large company

Lab Materials and Setup

- Pencil and paper

- Internet access

Getting Down to Business

Step 1 Define the acronym RAID and give a brief explanation of its function.

_____

_____

Step 2 What fault tolerance solutions are provided by the RAID standards? List and define each RAID standard that provides fault tolerance. If necessary, use the Internet to assist you in your research.

_____

_____

Step 3 What is the hardware requirement for each RAID fault tolerance standard that Windows 2000 supports?

_____

_____

Step 4 What RAID standard does not provide fault tolerance?

_____

_____

Step 5 What solution would you suggest be implemented for OV Investments?

_____

_____

Lab Analysis

1. In the Windows 2000 Computer Management console, there is a folder called Conflicts/ Sharing. What is this folder for? What can you do to resolve a device conflict?

    _____

    _____

2. What is the difference between hardware RAID and software RAID?

    _____

    _____

3. If you choose not to implement a RAID solution in your network, what other task can you complete to ensure that you have a secure copy of your data? What types of media are available for this solution?

    _____

    _____

4. Aside from implementing RAID and using other backup solutions, what other safeguards must you consider to provide reliability of data on your network?

    _____

    _____

5. What are COM ports and how do they relate to IRQs?

    _____

    _____

Key Term Quiz

Use the following vocabulary terms to complete the sentences below. Not all of the terms will be used.

digital audio tape (DAT)

digital linear tapes (DLTs)

disk duplexing

direct memory access (DMA)

disk mirroring

disk striping with parity

Enhanced Integrated Drive Electronics (EIDE) standard

interrupt request (IRQ)

macro

quarter-inch cartridge (QIC)

Small Computer System Interface (SCSI)

Trojan horse

universal asynchronous receiver-transmitter (UART)

1. _____ is the process of reading and writing data at the same time to two different hard drives through the use of two separate controllers for each drive.

2. The _____ is a special chip that takes digital serial data from a modem and converts it into parallel data that makes sense to the computer.

3. _____ are used to back up data and can have data capacities of up to 70 gigabytes.

4. Devices such as soundcards that use the _____ method of speeding up a device, talk directly to the RAM.

5. _____ viruses are programs that do something other than what they are expected to do.

Lab Wrap-Up

As you have seen, maintaining the perfect server requires knowing how your server devices talk to one another and what system resources are assigned to each device. Maintaining data integrity through fault tolerance solutions, such as RAID, are also tasks that are often necessary in today's network environments. You should now know the differences between the levels of RAID and the types of system resources that are available to devices on your computer.

Solutions

In this section, you'll find solutions to the lab exercises, the Lab Analysis questions, and the Key Term Quiz.

Lab 20.01 Solution

Step 1   The four system resources appear in Figure 20-1. They are direct memory access (DMA) channels, interrupt request line (IRQ) numbers, input/output (I/O) port addresses, and memory address ranges.

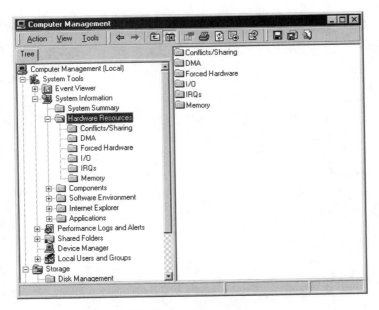

Figure 20-1 Hardware Resources

Step 2   The IRQs used will vary per computer. Figure 20-2 shows an example of the IRQ numbers and associated devices. IRQs are hardware lines over which devices can send signals to get the attention of the processor when the device is ready to accept or send information. Some IRQ numbers may not be listed, as they are not being used yet. IRQs are numbered from 0 to 15.

Step 3   DMA channels that are used will vary per computer. Figure 20-3 shows an example of the DMA channels and associated devices. There are seven DMA channels available for use on a personal computer. Of these seven channels, three are already reserved for use. Channels 0 and 4 are used by the computer's system and channel 2 is used by the floppy drive.

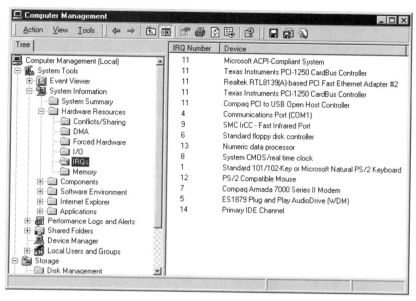

FIGURE 20-2 IRQs

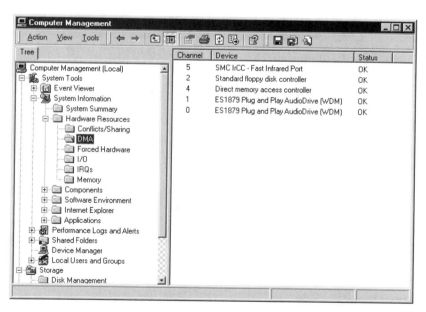

FIGURE 20-3 Direct memory access (DMA)

Step 4 An I/O port is a channel through which data is transferred between a device and the microprocessor. Figure 20-4 shows an example of the I/O ports and associated devices.

Step 5   A memory address is a portion of a computer's memory that can be allocated to an operating system, program, or device. Devices can be given a range of memory addresses. Figure 20-5 shows an example of the memory address ranges and associated devices.

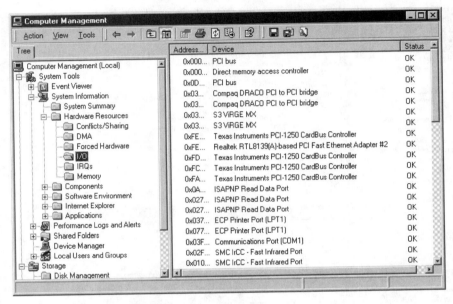

FIGURE 20-4 Input/output (I/O) port addresses

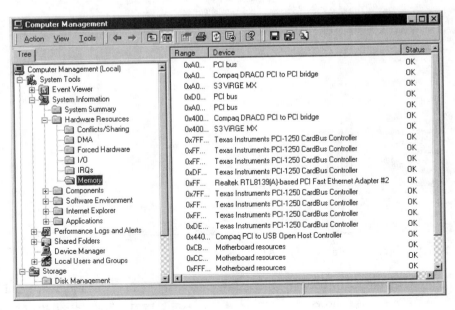

FIGURE 20-5 Memory addresses

Lab 20.02 Solution

Step 1   Redundant Array of Independent Disks (RAID) is a method that standardizes and categorizes fault tolerant disk systems. There are six levels of RAID, from level 0 to 5.

Step 2   The RAID standards are

- RAID 0—striped disk array (disk striping)

- RAID 1—disk mirroring and disk duplexing

- RAID 2—hamming code ECC

- RAID 3—parallel transfer with parity

- RAID 4—independent data disks with shared parity disk

- RAID 5—independent data disks with distributed parity blocks (disk striping with parity)

- RAID 6—independent data disks with two independent distributed parity schemes

You can find an excellent description of the advantages and disadvantages of each level of RAID, and the recommended applications of each level, at www.acnc.com/04_01_00.html.

Step 3   Windows 2000 supports a software implementation of RAID 0, 1, and 5.

Disk striping (RAID 0) requires that you spread the data across a minimum of two disk drives.

Disk mirroring (RAID 1) requires that you also have two disk drives, so that data can be written to both drives at the same time.

Disk duplexing (RAID 1) requires two separate drives and also two disk controllers to speed up the process of writing data to the drives. With the addition of another disk controller, the data does not have to be written twice by only one controller as is done in disk mirroring.

Disk striping with parity (RAID 5) must use at least three disk drives, and it is common that more than three are used. The data is stored on two drives and the parity information is written to the third disk drive.

Step 4   Disk striping (RAID 0) does not provide fault tolerance as the data is simply spread across at least two disk drives, so if one of the drives were to fail, you would lose all data on that disk.

Step 5   RAID 5 (disk striping with parity) provides the best fault tolerance solution as it provides the highest read data transaction rate and a medium write data transaction rate.

This solution does require a minimum of three disks, but OV Investments has indicated that there are no expense restrictions.

Answers to Lab Analysis

1. The Conflicts/Sharing folder is used to show any devices that are sharing resources or that are determined to have a conflict with other devices because they are attempting to use the same resource and are unable to do so. To resolve a device conflict, you can manually assign the resource settings for both devices to ensure that each setting is unique.

2. Software RAID is implemented through programs that run on the server. They usually support RAID 1 and RAID 5. They occupy the server's memory and CPU cycles so they can degrade overall performance on the server. Hardware RAID is implemented on a host-based RAID adapter and the array functions are tightly joined with the disk interface. The performance of hardware RAID is not dependent on the server CPU performance. Hardware arrays do not occupy any system memory and are not operating system dependent.

3. To maintain a secure copy of your data, nothing beats a tape backup. There are three main tape backup options: quarter-inch tape (QIC), digital audio tape (DAT), and digital linear tape (DLT).

4. Power problems will make all RAID and backup solutions irrelevant so you must consider implementing a dedicated circuit on your network so that devices on your network won't cause the power to sag. You should also look at implementing an uninterruptible power supply (UPS), surge protectors, and in the case of mission-critical environments, a backup power supply.

5. COM ports are preset combinations of I/O addresses and IRQs for serial connectors. These COM ports were defined to make device configuration easy. Each COM port has a related IRQ. For example COM1 and COM3 use IRQ4 and COM2 and COM4 use IRQ3.

Answers to Key Term Quiz

1. disk duplexing
2. universal asynchronous receiver-transmitter (UART)
3. digital linear tapes (DLTs)
4. direct memory access (DMA)
5. Trojan horse

Chapter 21

Zen and the Art of Network Support

Lab Exercises

When troubleshooting a network it is important to understand what tools are available to you and how to use these tools effectively to solve any problems that may occur. Planning a sequence of common troubleshooting steps may be helpful and save a great deal of time, as you can eliminate possible causes to problems one by one as you complete each step.

In this chapter, we will examine the Windows 2000 Performance console, which combines a few popular tools for monitoring systems. We will also look at the backup strategies available for keeping copies of your system data.

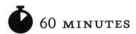 60 MINUTES

Lab 21.01: Using the Windows 2000 Performance Console

You have discovered that your server has been slowing down considerably in the past week. You need to determine the cause of the slowdown. You decide to monitor your server resources to determine if there are any bottlenecks.

Learning Objectives

In this lab, you'll examine the Performance console in Windows 2000. At the end of this lab, you will be able to

- Recognize the tools available for monitoring in the Performance console

- Use System Monitor to monitor server activity

- Analyze data to determine if bottlenecks exist

Lab Materials and Setup

For this lab exercise, you'll need

- Pencil and paper
- Internet access
- Windows 2000 Server or Advanced Server

Getting Down to Business

Step 1   From the Administrative Tools menu, select Performance. What tools are available in the Performance console for monitoring your server? Briefly list and describe each tool.

_____

_____

Step 2   Select the System Monitor object. From the System Monitor toolbar, click the Add Counters icon. In the Add Counters window, ensure that your server is present in the Select Counters From Computer field. From the Performance Object drop-down menu, select Processor. In the Select Counters From List box, select % Processor Time. Click the Add button. What does the % Processor Time counter indicate?

_____

_____

Step 3   From the Performance Object drop-down menu, select PhysicalDisk. Click the Add button. In the Select Counters From List box, select % Disk Time. What does the % Disk Time counter indicate?

_____

_____

Step 4   From the Performance Object drop-down menu, select Memory. Click the Add button. In the Select Counters From List box, select Pages/sec. What does the Pages/sec counter indicate?

_____

_____

Step 5   Click Close to close the Add Counters window. The System Monitor appears with activity evident in the chart.

Step 6   Leave the Performance console window open. From the Run command, type **winnt\ system32\freecell.exe**.

Step 7   The FreeCell game appears. Play the game for several seconds. Return to the Performance console.

Step 8   Click the Freeze Display icon from the System Monitor toolbar. Analyze the counter data that is shown for each object. Are there any bottlenecks evident? If so, list them and explain what the levels are, compared to what the levels should be for each counter.

_____

_____

 60 MINUTES

Lab 21.02: Comparing Backup Strategies

Karayanis Cookies needs to maintain a copy of all product orders. They have a server on their network that maintains the data daily, but they know that they won't have enough space on this server to keep order data for any more than one day at a time. They wish to implement a backup strategy and have asked you to suggest some options for them. Karayanis Cookies has indicated to you that they wish the backups to be done at night when the product orders are at a minimum. They also wish to minimize backup time and are not concerned about the time to restore a backup.

Learning Objectives

In this lab, you'll suggest a backup strategy for a small company. At the end of this lab, you will be able to

- List and define the backup strategies available

- Recommend a backup solution for Karayanis Cookies

Lab Materials and Setup

For this lab exercise, you'll need

- Pencil and paper

- Internet access

Getting Down to Business

Step 1 What backup strategies can you suggest to Karayanis Cookies? List and describe each backup strategy. Use the Internet to assist you in your research, if necessary.

Step 2   Based on the restrictions that Karayanis Cookies has mentioned to you, what backup strategy would meet their requirements? Why?

_____

_____

✔ **Hint**

You can combine backup strategies to best meet the needs of the company.

Step 3   Would the restore time for this backup strategy meet their requirements? Briefly give a reason for your answer.

_____

_____

Step 4   How many backup tapes would you need to restore a backup strategy of this type for one five-day period?

_____

_____

Lab Analysis

1. Besides the tools available in the Windows 2000 Performance console, what other common software troubleshooting tools are available for your network?

    _____

    _____

2. Once you've successfully backed up a system, where should you store the backup tapes?

    _____

    _____

3. What are the four main subsystems on a server that you should monitor?

    _____

    _____

4. When configuring a Performance Alert, what actions can you configure to occur once the threshold has been reached?

    _____

    _____

5. When establishing a troubleshooting model for a system or network, what steps should you include?

    _____

    _____

Key Term Quiz

Use the following vocabulary terms to complete the sentences below. Not all of the terms will be used.

baseline

broadcast storm

counter

NetWare Loadable Module (NLM)

network monitor

object

system log

system management software suites

1. A(n) _____ in System Monitor is the component of your system you want to monitor, such as the disk or the processor.

2. When monitoring your server's activity, it is best to compare any data gathered with a _____ that you have established when your server was working correctly.

3. A dying network card can often produce a large number of packets, known as a _____.

4. One Novell program that runs on the server, which you can use to monitor the server remotely from a client computer, is called _____.

5. The _____, found in Windows 2000 Event Viewer, displays any errors or problems that have occurred on your server.

Lab Wrap-Up

Congratulations! You have successfully completed all of the labs in this manual. Take a moment to pat yourself on the back and then rush right out to put the knowledge and troubleshooting skills that you have acquired to good use in your network environment.

Remember, a computer network is a great way of sharing data with others; however, it has to be maintained daily, so best of luck with your network endeavors!

Solutions

In this section, you'll find solutions to the lab exercises, the Lab Analysis questions, and the Key Term Quiz.

Lab 21.01 Solution

Step 1   Figure 21-1 shows the tools available for monitoring a server. They are

- System Monitor tool charts real-time activity and displays information about the counters and objects that you choose to monitor.

- Performance Logs and Alerts records and logs server activity over a period of time. You can configure alerts to track system activity and inform a user, start a process or record the information to a log when a counter exceeds the thresholds defined.

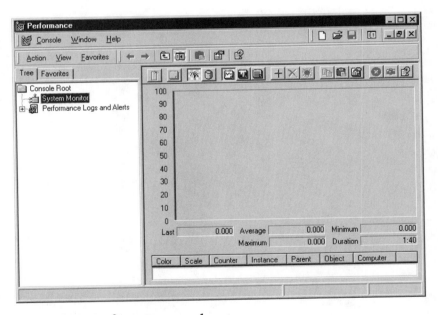

Figure 21-1   Performance console

Step 2   The % Processor Time counter, shown in Figure 21-2, indicates the percentage of time that the processor is running non-idle threads.

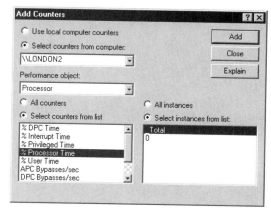

Figure 21-2 Processor object

Step 3 The % Disk Time counter, shown in Figure 21-3, indicates the percentage of time that a hard drive is reading or writing data.

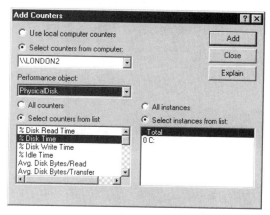

Figure 21-3 PhysicalDisk object

Step 4 The Pages/sec counter, shown in Figure 21-4, indicates the total in and out paging activity, such as when a program references data that is not in its physical memory.

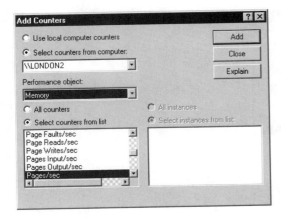

FIGURE 21-4 Memory object

Step 5   Figure 21-5 shows the active System Monitor.

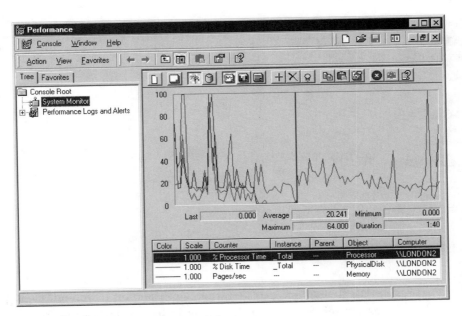

FIGURE 21-5 System Monitor activity

Step 6   Ensure that the correct path is typed in the Run command window as shown in Figure 21-6.

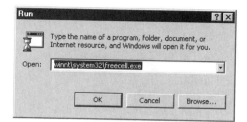

FIGURE 21-6 Run command

Step 7   Ensure that the FreeCell game appears, as shown in Figure 21-7.

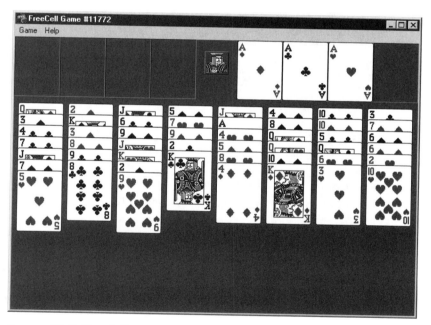

FIGURE 21-7 FreeCell game

Step 8   Ensure that the System Monitor display is frozen, as shown in Figure 21-8.

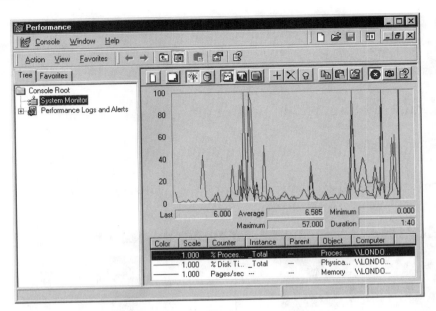

FIGURE 21-8 Freeze display in System Monitor

Answers will vary according to the computer; however, the acceptable ranges for each counter are

% Processor Time   Below 20 percent indicates that the server is underutilized and/or services may not be running. A consistent value above 70 percent indicates a bottleneck with the server.

% Disk Time   A consistent value over 90 percent indicates that there is a bottleneck with the hard drive of the server.

Pages/sec   A consistent value over ten indicates that there is a memory bottleneck.

Lab 21.01 Solution

Step 1   The different types of backups available for Karayanis Cookies are

Full/Normal   The entire database/server is backed up each time that you perform this process. The Archive bit will be turned off for every file backed up. This is time consuming when backing up and restoring.

Incremental   Only data that has changed since the last backup is captured in this backup. This requires other members of a backup set to accurately restore all data to the server. The

Archive bits are turned off after the backup is complete. This can be a very fast backup and a slower restore, as all parts of the backup set need to be applied in a restore.

Differential All data that has changed since the last full backup is captured in this backup. Archive bits are not turned off. This can be a very slow backup and a quicker restore.

Copy Identical to a Full/Normal backup except that the Archive bits are turned on. This is used to make copies of a previously completed back up. This is time consuming when backing up and restoring.

Daily or Daily/Copy This is the backup of all files changed that day. This does not turn off the Archive bits. This can be a quick backup and quick restore, but requires other members of the backup set.

Step 2 A Full/Normal with Incremental backup strategy will meet the requirements of Karayanis Cookies. A Full/Normal backup could be done once a week and Incremental backups could be done daily. A Full/Normal backup would back up all data, and the daily Incremental backups would back up the data that has changed only on that particular day.

Step 3 The restore time would meet their time restrictions, as they have asked that the backup time be kept to a minimum and they are not concerned about the time it would take to restore the backup set. Incremental backups will minimize the nightly backup time as only that particular day's changes are backed up. Any data that has not changed is not backed up.

Step 4 For a five-day period, Karayanis Cookies would require one Full/Normal backup tape and four daily Incremental tapes to restore the server to full integrity.

Answers to Lab Analysis

1. Common software troubleshooting tools include protocol or network analyzers, system logs, and system management software suites.

2. Backup tapes should always be stored off-site in a secure location for their protection.

3. Network, disk, memory, and processor are the four main subsystems on a server that should be monitored regularly.

4. When configuring a Performance Alert, you can specify the following actions to occur once the threshold is met:

   - Log an entry in the Application event log

   - Send a network message to a computer system

   - Start performance data log

   - Run a program

5. The basics of any troubleshooting model should include the following steps:

   a) Establish the symptoms.

   b) Isolate the cause of the problem (identify the scope of the problem).

   c) Establish what has changed that might have caused the problem.

   d) Identify the most probable cause.

   e) Implement a solution.

   f) Test the solution.

   g) Recognize the potential effects of the solution.

   h) Document the solution.

Answers to Key Term Quiz

1. object

2. baseline

3. broadcast storm

4. NetWare Loadable Module (NLM)

5. system log

Index

INTERNATIONAL CONTACT INFORMATION

AUSTRALIA
McGraw-Hill Book Company Australia Pty. Ltd.
TEL +61-2-9417-9899
FAX +61-2-9417-5687
http://www.mcgraw-hill.com.au
books-it_sydney@mcgraw-hill.com

CANADA
McGraw-Hill Ryerson Ltd.
TEL +905-430-5000
FAX +905-430-5020
http://www.mcgrawhill.ca

GREECE, MIDDLE EAST,
NORTHERN AFRICA
McGraw-Hill Hellas
TEL +30-1-656-0990-3-4
FAX +30-1-654-5525

MEXICO (Also serving Latin America)
McGraw-Hill Interamericana Editores S.A. de C.V.
TEL +525-117-1583
FAX +525-117-1589
http://www.mcgraw-hill.com.mx
fernando_castellanos@mcgraw-hill.com

SINGAPORE (Serving Asia)
McGraw-Hill Book Company
TEL +65-863-1580
FAX +65-862-3354
http://www.mcgraw-hill.com.sg
mghasia@mcgraw-hill.com

SOUTH AFRICA
McGraw-Hill South Africa
TEL +27-11-622-7512
FAX +27-11-622-9045
robyn_swanepoel@mcgraw-hill.com

UNITED KINGDOM & EUROPE
(Excluding Southern Europe)
McGraw-Hill Education Europe
TEL +44-1-628-502500
FAX +44-1-628-770224
http://www.mcgraw-hill.co.uk
computing_neurope@mcgraw-hill.com

ALL OTHER INQUIRIES Contact:
Osborne/McGraw-Hill
TEL +1-510-549-6600
FAX +1-510-883-7600
http://www.osborne.com
omg_international@mcgraw-hill.com

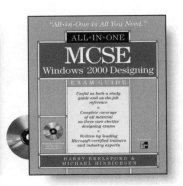
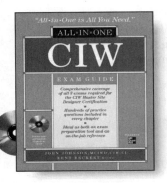

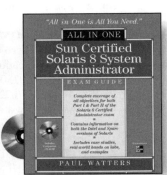